D1201132

THE ORCHESTRA
ORCHESTRAL TECHNIQUES
AND COMBINATIONS

Ebenezer Prout

DOVER PUBLICATIONS, INC.
Mineola, New York

Bibliographical Note

This Dover edition, first published in 2003, is an unabridged republication of *The Orchestra, Volume II: Orchestral Combinations,* first published by Augener & Co., London, in 1889.

Library of Congress Cataloging-in-Publication Data

Prout, Ebenezer, 1835–1909.
    The orchestra : orchestral techniques and combinations / Ebenezer Prout.
        p. cm.
    Originally published as v. 2 of: The orchestra. London : Augener & Co., c1899.
    ISBN 0-486-42851-6 (pbk.)
    1. Instrumentation and orchestration. I. Title.

MT70.P966 2003
784.13'7—dc21

2003043997

Manufactured in the United States of America
Dover Publications, Inc., 31 East 2nd Street, Mineola, N.Y. 11501

PREFACE.

——◆×◆——

WITH the present volume the subject of Instrumentation is completed. After what was said in the preface to the first volume of this work, no lengthy remarks will be needful here.

The first thing to be said is, that here, more than in any other volume of this series, it has been necessary to teach by example. It will be seen, therefore, that the quotations from orchestral scores occupy a far larger portion of the space than the letter-press. Merely to talk about combinations of instruments, without giving actual illustrations, would have been absolutely useless to the student. As in the preceding volume, the passages selected have been taken from works of the most varied style, and of different periods, from the time of Haydn down to the present day. With the exception of two passages by Bach and Handel in Chapter VII., illustrating the employment of the organ, no examples have been quoted anterior to Haydn ; for it is with this composer that the modern science of orchestration may be said to begin. Though a few well-known extracts will be found among the illustrations, special effort has been made to avoid, as far as possible, hackneyed quotations, and the author believes that the very large majority of the examples given will be new to the greater number of his readers.

With a view of systematizing the teaching as far as possible, the stringed orchestra is first dealt with ; this subject is comparatively so simple that its treatment presented but little difficulty. In the following chapter, the management of the wind instruments—a much more complicated subject—is spoken of. To do anything like justice to this question, a large number of illustrations were absolutely necessary.

Students are so apt to imagine that, in order to produce any adequate results, it is necessary to use a large number of instruments, that it was thought advisable to give a chapter on the treatment of the 'small orchestra,' in order to show how much was possible with this alone. It is hoped that the many charming, and mostly unfamiliar passages quoted in this chapter may lead the young musician to see the beauty of moderation in the use of his resources.

The two following chapters, on ' Balance of Tone,' and ' Contrast and Colour,' were at the same time the most difficult, and the most fascinating to write, of the whole volume. There is no mistake which beginners are so prone to make as that of balancing their parts badly, especially in a *tutti* ; at the same time, there is no part of orchestral writing in which practical experience is more necessary. The chapter devoted to this subject is therefore one of the longest in the volume. Yet the author does not flatter himself that he has dealt with it adequately ; nothing beyond the most general principles could be laid down. Only careful analysis by the student of the examples quoted can give the necessary guidance in this most important matter.

Hardly less is the case with the chapter on ' Contrast and Colour.' The latter, especially, is so essentially a question of personal feeling and taste on the part of the composer, that all that has been possible has been to endeavour to stimulate his imagination, by setting before him a large number of models of the most varied kinds, showing him some of the innumerable possibilities of the modern orchestra.

The chapter on ' The Combination of the Organ with the Orchestra' deals with a subject on which, so far as the author is aware, very little has been written. It is hoped that the numerous examples quoted will be found of assistance to the student. In the following chapter, the important question of ' Orchestral Accompaniment' is dealt with as fully as space allowed.

The arrangement of music for the orchestra is a matter which offers considerable difficulty to most students, owing to the large amount of textual alteration which is often necessary. In order to teach this, the author has thought it best, first to take a few representative pianoforte passages, and to score them for orchestra, explaining as fully as he could the reasons why a particular course has been adopted ; and then to give some passages for the piano which eminent composers have themselves scored. Here, again, it has been impossible to lay down rules applicable in all cases. A short chapter follows, in which some hints are given as to scoring for incomplete orchestras.

It was the author's original intention to treat the subject of Chamber Music, to which the final chapter is devoted, at much greater length than has been found possible within the limits of this volume, and, as in other parts of the work, to give copious examples. The exigencies of space absolutely forbade this ; and nothing more than general principles have been given, which may, it is thought, be found serviceable. Here, as in the rest of this volume, the student must supplement what is wanting by careful examination of the works of the great masters.

Nobody can be more conscious than the author of the short-comings of the present treatise. The subject is so vast, and so impossible to exhaust, that he feels keenly how much remains to be said. Happily it is possible for the student to supplement for himself the instructions here given. Orchestration cannot possibly be learned solely from books on the subject; long and careful study of scores, and the hearing of orchestral music, are absolutely necessary adjuncts. But the present work will at least serve to guide the learner as to the direction which his own studies should take ; the rest he must do for himself.

As in the first volume, the author would again acknowledge his obligations to his predecessors in the same field. He has, as before, found much assistance from M. Gevaert's treatise, so often referred to, and he has also taken some valuable hints, especially for the final chapter, from the fourth volume of Marx's 'Composition'—the only work he has met with which deals with the subject of Chamber Music.

Once again, the author has to thank his friends Professor Mahaffy and Dr. C. W. Pearce for their kind assistance in correcting the proof-sheets, and his pupil, Mr. J. Spawforth, for the preparation of the analytical index.

It is with great thankfulness that the author completes with this volume the series of theoretical works which for the last eleven years have occupied so much of his time and thoughts. Many of his happiest hours have been spent in the writing of these volumes ; and the reception they have met with, both in this country and abroad, has proved to him that he has not laboured in vain, nor spent his strength for naught. The benefit that he has reason to believe that students have derived from the series has more than repaid him for all the labour spent in its preparation.

London : February, 1899.

TABLE OF CONTENTS.

CHAPTER IV.—THE SMALL ORCHESTRA ... ... *page* 55

CHAPTER V.—BALANCE OF TONE ... ... *page* 81

THE ORCHESTRA.

PART II.—ORCHESTRAL COMBINATION.

CHAPTER I.

INTRODUCTION.

1. In the preceding volume of this work the nature and capabilities of all the instruments employed in the modern orchestra were treated of, and it was said, in concluding this part of the subject, that much still remained to be taught. To refer once more to the analogy of painting, frequently mentioned in the first volume, it may be said that the student who knows no more than he has learned from that volume is in much the same condition as a young artist would be, who had provided himself with a large box of colours, and who knew the exact shade of each colour separately, but who had only very vague notions as to how they should be mixed. It is the proper method of mixing his orchestral colours which it is the object of the present volume to teach—so far at least, as it is possible to teach it from a book. But the difficulties in the way of imparting this knowledge are far greater than those hitherto met with. For, while it is possible to give very definite rules as to what is practicable or impracticable on any instrument, the combinations of the different instruments with one another are absolutely inexhaustible; and so much depends on the individual feeling and taste of the composer, that the utmost that can be done is, to lay down some general principles for his guidance, and to illustrate these, and at the same time to stimulate his imagination, by placing before him numerous examples from the works of the great masters of orchestration.

2. To a certain extent, the two parts into which we have divided the present work—Technique and Combination—may be said to overlap one another. In the illustrations that we gave in the preceding volume, numerous examples of combination were seen, and some of these were explained and commented upon in the text. We now propose to enter more systematically into the discussion of various matters hitherto only incidentally touched upon, as well as of others which have been hardly, if at all, mentioned.

3. The student already knows that the instruments of the orchestra are of three kinds—strings, wind, and percussion ; and, in order to simplify his studies, we shall deal with these separately, before treating of the orchestra as a whole. The percussion instruments, however, will not require separate treatment, as they are very rarely used by themselves for more than a few notes.* But both the strings and the wind are frequently employed alone ; and we shall first examine the works of the great composers, and try to deduce from their practice some general hints for the guidance of the student.

4. Having considered the treatment of strings and wind separately, we shall next show how to combine them. Here, again, our subject divides into two parts—the small orchestra and the full orchestra. By the former, of which we shall first speak, is meant an orchestra without percussion instruments, and with no brass excepting horns. Many very fine works exist for the small orchestra,—it will suffice to refer to Mozart's immortal symphony in G minor as showing how much effect can be produced, even from the point of view of the orchestration, with limited means. The slow movement of Beethoven's symphony in D, the *allegretto* of his symphony in F, and the first two movements of his Pastoral symphony, afford other illustrations of the same point.

5. When we reach the full orchestra, a most important question will present itself—that of the balance of tone. There is, perhaps, hardly any matter in connection with instrumentation in which the beginner is more likely to go astray, and there are few, unfortunately, concerning which it is more difficult to lay down more than very general rules. A somewhat detailed examination of passages by the great masters will be necessary ; but this alone will not suffice. Practical experience, and learning by the failures of his early attempts, will be almost a necessity for the student here.

6. No less important than balance of tone are the subjects which will next engage our attention—Contrast and Colour. Here, again, are matters on which explicit directions, or hard and fast rules, are impossible. We can only teach by examples ; the student's natural ability and feeling must do the rest. A chapter on the combination of the organ with the orchestra will conclude this part of our subject.

7. After having dealt with the orchestra as an independent body, we shall treat of its employment for the purpose of accompaniment, both of solos (whether instrumental or vocal) and of choral music. We shall then speak of the arrangement for the orchestra of music originally written for the piano or organ. This is a matter in which an inexperienced student often makes grave

---

* As, for instance, in Exs. 193, 195, 196, and 200 of the first volume of this work.

mistakes; happily, it is easier here than in some other parts of this volume to lay down definite principles for his guidance.

8. In many places, especially in provincial theatres, small and incomplete orchestras are to be found. It will probably be useful to give a few hints as to scoring for such combinations as are likely to be met with. A chapter will therefore be devoted to this subject, though it will obviously be impossible to deal with half the cases likely to be found. At the most, only a few guiding principles can possibly be given.

9. With the view of making this work as complete as possible, a chapter will be added on the scoring of chamber music. Properly speaking, this scarcely belongs to "orchestration" in the strict sense of the term; but in no other volume of the series could the subject be suitably treated, as the technique of the instruments had not been previously explained.

10. Before proceeding further, the author would earnestly warn students against expecting too much from the present book. It has been already said that on many points nothing beyond the most general principles can be given; and under no circumstances can orchestration be learned simply from a book. The student is likely to derive far more benefit from a careful analysis of th examples here given from the great masters than from the most assiduous study of the text.

CHAPTER II.

THE STRINGED ORCHESTRA.

11. We said in the preceding volume that the stringed instruments were the groundwork of the modern orchestra; and in §§ 55–57 the reasons were given why this must necessarily be the case. Formerly many works were composed for stringed instruments alone; we need only name Handel's 'Twelve Grand Concertos' and the 'Concerti Grossi' of Corelli as examples. At the present time comparatively little is written for the stringed orchestra, though Grimm, Volkmann, Wüerst, and others have composed Suites for strings alone. It is nevertheless so important that the student should know how to write well for strings, that we must enter at some length into the subject before speaking of the orchestra as a whole.

12. Owing to the general similarity in the quality of tone of stringed instruments, far less variety of colour is possible, in writing for them alone, than when they are combined or alternated with wind instruments. True, there is a perceptible difference between the tone of the violin and of the viola, and still more between that of the violin and of the upper register of the violoncello; but the difference is far less than that existing between any stringed instrument and, let us say, a clarinet or a horn. When, therefore, contrast is required from the strings, it is sought for by variety of rhythm, and by other devices which will be shown in our examples.

13. As a general rule (though, as we shall see presently, there are numerous exceptions), music for the strings is written in four parts, the lowest part—that of the violoncellos—being doubled in the octave below by the double-basses. While in most cases the melody is given to the first violins, the alto part of the harmony to the second violins, the tenor to the violas, and the bass to the celli, with or without the double-bass, crossing of the parts is much more freely used than in vocal writing. In general the student may cross his parts whenever he finds it convenient to do so for the sake of the purity of his part-writing. But there is one limitation to this general permission. Owing to the penetrating and incisive tone of the upper notes of the violoncello, that instrument should not be written above the viola or violins, except for a special melodic effect. (See Vol. I., Ex. 42.) The crossing

of which we are now speaking refers chiefly to the three upper
string parts.

14. The first question to be considered is the *position* of the
harmony.   Here the general rules for vocal part-writing apply,
though exceptions, not only to this, but probably to every other
rule we shall give in this volume, are to be found in the works of
the great composers.   It must not be forgotten that we do not
profess to do more than to lay down general principles, the application of which may be subject to many modifications.   It is
mostly not good to have too wide an interval between two adjacent
parts, especially between the two upper or the two middle parts.
The following passage shows a good distribution of the strings.

Observe here how the low G of the double-bass is reinforced in
the upper octave by the violoncello on the first crotchet of each
bar.

15. Our next example shows some wider intervals between the parts.

The chief point to notice here is, that from the fourth bar onwards the violoncellos replace the violas, because the counterpoint which the composer here requires goes below the compass of the latter instrument. The wide intervals—nearly two octaves in bar 5— between the cello and the double-bass do not here produce a bad effect, because the double-bass has a sustained pedal note. A moving bass part not doubled in the octave above would have been less good.

16. It was said above (§ 12), that contrast in writing for strings was mostly obtained by variety of rhythms.   Our next quotation will illustrate this point.

Ex. 3.

Here three kinds of contrast are seen—that of the moving semi-quavers of the violas with the sustained harmony of the violins and cello, that of the violins *con sordini* as against the other strings without mutes, and the pizzicato of the double basses against the *arco* of the other strings.   The separation of the double basses from the violoncellos is far more common, and more effective in a *piano*, as here, than in a *forte*.

17. Frequently, especially in quiet passages, the double-basses are silent, and the bass is given to the violoncellos alone.   The commencement of one of Haydn's least-known symphonies furnishes a good example of this.

Ex. 4.

The first chord here is also played by the wind instruments—flute, oboes, bassoons, and horns—which it is needless to quote. Note the position of the first chord, as illustrating what was said in § 14.

18. Occasionally, for a special effect, the usual distribution of the string parts (§ 13) is changed.

Gluck : 'Iphigénie en Aulide.'

Ex. 5.

Andante.

Fagotti.

Viol. 1.

Viol. 2.

Viola.

Here the bass of the harmony is given to the first violins, doubled in the first two bars by the violas, while the second violins have the top part. Observe also, as bearing on the important question of balance of tone, with which we shall deal later, that at the third bar the violas are reinforced by the first bassoon, in order to bring the middle part of the harmony into due prominence.

19. If the composer wishes to write a passage—whether scale, arpeggio, or other melodic design—which exceeds the compass of

one instrument, and has to be, so to speak, "handed along" from one to another, it is best, in order to secure a smooth connection, to let the newly entering part begin *on, and not after*, the last note of the preceding instrument.   A good example of this will be seen in the Scherzo of Mendelssohn's 'Midsummer Night's Dream' music, just before the return of the first subject, where a chromatic scale of four octaves is divided between the strings. We give a less familiar illustration of the same procedure.

Ex. 6.   NICOLAI : 'Die lustigen Weiber von Windsor.'

20. Our next illustration shows the melody given to the violoncelli, and accompanied by repeated notes, given alternately to the double-basses and the three upper string parts.

Ex. 7.   SCHUBERT : 'Alfonso und Estrella.'

21. In speaking of the pizzicato in our preceding volume (§ 87), the student was warned against writing too rapid passages to be played in this manner. The following extract shows not only a most effective use of the pizzicato, but gives approximately the limit of rapidity advisable.

Ex. 8. *Allegretto.*   DELIBES : 'Sylvia.'

This passage is instructive in more than one respect. **Note first** the disposition of the harmony, with the occasional crossing, for a single chord, of the violas and the violoncellos. Observe, also, particularly how careful the composer has been in writing his double-stops and chords. All are perfectly easy, and can be played either in the first or third position.

22. Though the strings are mostly written in four-part harmony, we often find passages in which, for the sake of variety or contrast, fewer than four parts are employed. We have seen one instance of this in Ex. 5, and many others may easily be found. Sometimes the harmony is in only two parts, as in the opening of the finale of Mozart's so-called 'Parisian' symphony.

Ex. 9.　　Mozart: Symphony in D, No. 31.

23. Harmony in two parts is at other times given to all the strings, one or both parts being doubled in the octave, as in the following passage:

Ex. 10.　　Haydn: Symphony in E flat.

24. What are commonly called 'unison' passages for the strings—that is, passages in which all the strings are playing in unison *and octaves*, are so common that no example is needed. In such cases, the violins mostly play in unison, the violoncellos an octave below them, while the violas double in unison either the former or the latter, according to the pitch of the passage. Sometimes, however, the distribution is different. Let the student look at the Presto of Beethoven's third 'Leonora' overture. Here the first violins begin alone; at the ninth bar the second violins double them in the lower octave; then the violas enter, and last the violoncellos and basses, each an octave lower than the preceding part, till at last the tumultuous figure

is heard in five octaves.

25. On the other hand, the difference in pitch of the various stringed instruments renders the *actual* unison very rare; and if it is employed, it is necessary to suppress the double-basses. We saw in Ex. 46 of the preceding volume that when the violin and violoncello were playing in unison, the first string of the latter corresponded in pitch to the fourth string of the former. Obviously it would be impracticable to write for the double-bass in unison with the violin. A fine example of the effect of which we are now speaking is found in Meyerbeer's 'L'Africaine.'

Ex. 11. *Andante cantabile.*   MEYERBEER: 'L'Africaine.'

Here we see, not only the whole mass of the strings, except the double-basses, but a further reinforcement of their power by the addition of the clarinets and bassoons. The low notes of the clarinets add a soft and mellow tint to the combination.

26. For a quiet accompaniment to a solo, sometimes only a part of the strings are employed. In the great scena in the second act of 'Der Freischütz,' the opening bars of the *adagio* are accompanied only by divided violins and violas. We give an example by Weber accompanied by violas and celli, both divided.

Spare,   oh   spare   yon ten - der.... flower!

Observe here that the upper part of the harmony is given, not to
the first viola, but to the first violoncello, the quality of its tone
being much richer.   Mendelssohn has imitated this combination
in the opening of the duet " My song shall be alway Thy mercy,"
in the ' Lobgesang.'

27. It is not uncommon to find some of the strings divided for
part, or the whole of a movement.   This is perhaps most frequently
the case with the violas.   We give a charming example by Mozart.

Ex. 13.   MOZART: Symphony in C, No. 34.

Andante di molto.

Viol. 1.

Viol. 2.

Violá 1.

Viola 2.

Bassi.

&c.

28. We now give a few instances of rarer, but effective and interesting combinations of strings. Our first is the Evocation of the Spirit of the Alps, in Schumann's music to ' Manfred.'

Here the melody is given to the first violins *con sordini,* while the divided second violins and the two violas are without mutes, and are doubled in the unison by the flutes and clarinets. Notice the effect of the single harmonic of the harp on the third beat of each bar.

29. Our next example

shows a tenor solo, accompanied by violas, two celli (*soli*) and double-basses, and echoed by muted violins in octaves—a novel and beautiful combination.

30. In our last two quotations have been seen examples of the incidental employment of solo strings. Occasionally only a single stringed instrument is used in each part. A tolerably familiar instance of this will be seen in the finale of Beethoven's Choral Fantasia, Op. 80. We give a short passage from Gounod's 'Faust,' in which the composer required an especially delicate accompaniment for the voices, and therefore employs a solo quartet.

31. In Ex. 8 we gave an instance of the treatment of all the strings *pizzicato*. We now give another example of the same device, in which the stringed orchestra is designed to imitate a guitar. It is the beginning of Mephistopheles's mocking serenade in Berlioz's 'Faust'; and a very novel effect is here obtained by the wide arpeggios of the second violin and viola. These could hardly be played in the usual manner; Berlioz in his score directs the performers to glide the thumb rapidly across the four strings.

Ex. 17. *Tempo di Valse.*   BERLIOZ : 'La Damnation de Faust.'

32. It is quite impossible within the limits at our disposal to indicate, much less to quote, more than a small number of the possible effects to be obtained from the strings alone. For our final examples we give two passages in which very full harmony is obtained by the division of the strings. The first is a very quiet and rather sombre effect from Gounod's Cecilian Mass.

Ex. 18. *Adagio.* GOUNOD : Messe Solennelle.

In such passages as this, it is very seldom that the writing is in eight *real* parts ; mostly, as here, the parts are doubled in the octave.

33. Our final example is quite different.

Here we have five-part harmony ; and a strange and very unusual effect is obtained by the *f* and *ff* for the muted strings. The mutes are almost invariably employed only for quiet passages. It need hardly be said that the volume of tone, even with a large orchestra, will be very greatly diminished, first by the division of the parts, and secondly by the employment of the mutes.

34. In concluding this chapter, a word should be said as to the difference of effect of the various keys on the stringed instruments. Though it is easy for the imagination to exaggerate this difference, there can be no doubt that it really exists, and may be easily explained. Our readers are presumably acquainted with what is known as "sympathetic resonance." (See *Applied Forms*, §§ 24–26.) In virtue of the law there explained, the open strings of a stringed instrument vibrate in unison with a note sounded in their vicinity, provided that such note is either their fundamental tone, or one of their upper partials. Consequently if a violin is played in a key containing in its scale the notes of its open strings, or the earlier upper partials of those notes, its power will be more or less reinforced by the sympathetic resonance of the other strings. For this reason keys which have not more than four sharps are more brilliant than the extreme sharp keys, and in general sharp keys are more brilliant than flat. As an illustration of this point, it may be mentioned that Berlioz, in arranging Weber's 'Invitation à la Valse' for the orchestra, transposed it from D flat to D major, partly, perhaps, for technical reasons, but chiefly, no doubt, because it was a far more brilliant and favourable key for the strings. We can recall no example of any brilliant orchestral movement being written in the key of A flat, though E flat is not uncommon, as, for instance, in Mozart's overture to 'Die Zauberflöte,' Weber's to 'Euryanthe, and Auber's to 'Le Cheval de Bronze.'

CHAPTER III.

THE TREATMENT OF WIND INSTRUMENTS.

35. Owing to the many kinds of wind instruments employed in the orchestra, and the different qualities of their tone, an infinitely larger number of combinations is possible with them than with the stringed instruments with which we dealt in the last chapter. There is, indeed, practically no limit to the variety of tone-colour that may be obtained by wind instruments alone; and it will be impossible for us to do more than to enunciate a few general principles for the guidance of the student, and to enforce them by examples taken from works of different composers and of different schools.

36. Wind instruments, when employed alone, may be treated in two ways—either as solo instruments or in masses. In the former case, sometimes one instrument has the melody, and the others give simply an accompaniment; at other times several instruments are, so to speak, individualized as soloists. When treated in masses, no one instrument comes into special prominence, and the effect is obtained by their combination on approximately equal terms. We shall proceed to give examples of both methods, commencing with the treatment of wind instruments in solo passages.

37. Our first illustration

Ex. 20.   MENDELSSOHN: 'Lauda Sion.'

shows a solo oboe accompanied only by two clarinets; until the cadence, where the strings enter, the harmony is in three parts.

38. Our next example has two or three points calling for remark.

Notice first the order of the score. In compositions written, like this Notturno, for wind instruments alone, the bassoons are not infrequently placed below the horns, as here. The same arrangement will be found in Mozart's numerous Serenades and Divertimenti for wind instruments only. The reason is, that in such works the real bass of the harmony is usually given to the bassoons, and it is therefore convenient that they should have the lowest staff or staves of the score.

39. It is rare to find an important solo passage given to the C clarinet, which is inferior in tone to those in B and A. This work was written early in the present century, when C clarinets were much more frequently used than now. Players at the present day would probably transpose the whole movement for the B clarinet. From the fifth bar of the above extract, there are *two* solo instruments, the first clarinet being imitated by the first horn.

40. It is not needful that the solo should always be in the upper part. Our next example shows the melody in the tenor given to the first bassoon.

Ex. 22. BEETHOVEN : Sextett, Op. 71.

41. In the following striking passage, from the second finale of 'Die Zauberflöte,'

Ex. 23. MOZART : 'Die Zauberflöte.'

we see a flute solo accompanied by the whole mass of the brass *piano.* Observe that the contrast of tone here between the melody and the accompaniment is more strongly marked than in the preceding examples. Note also the numerous rests given to the brass. If these instruments had had sustained chords written for them, the effect of the flute solo would have been much impaired.

42. Sometimes several wind instruments of different quality are all combined as solo instruments. Almost infinite variety is obtainable in this way. We give two examples.

Ex. 24. *Sostenuto assai.*   CHERUBINI : Mass in D.

This beautiful passage—the opening symphony of the " Et incarnatus "— is so simple as to need no comment.

43. Our next illustration, quite different in style, is the commencement of the overture to ' Zanetta.'

Ex. 25. *Allegretto.*   Auber : 'Zanetta.

44. Though in the majority of cases we find in such examples as those just quoted that the upper part of the harmony is given to the instrument which stands highest in the score, it is not uncommon to find this order departed from, as in the following passage :

Ex. 26. *Adagio sostenuto assai.*
Liszt: Piano Concerto in A.

Here the melody is given to the first clarinet, and the first flute has one of the middle parts of the harmony.

45. The passage just quoted illustrates a somewhat important point. The A in the middle of the harmony is given to the flute, not to the oboe. If chords of a smooth and homogeneous quality of tone are desired from the wood, it is in most cases better to omit the oboes from the combination. The tone of the oboe is so reedy, incisive, and penetrating, that it amalgamates with the other instruments with difficulty, and always obtrudes its personality more or less. It was doubtless for this reason that Mozart, when he added clarinets to the score of his great symphony in G minor, rewrote the original oboe parts, and in nearly all the passages for wind alone replaced them by the clarinets. As the score of the revised version of the symphony is very little known—it is, we believe, published only in the complete edition of Mozart's works —we give the last bars of the minuet as an illustration.

Ex. 27.
Allegretto.
Mozart: Symphony in G minor, No. 40.

Let the student try to hear mentally the clarinet parts, first with oboe tone as originally written, and then as here given, and he cannot fail to notice how much smoother the blending of the instruments is in the latter case than in the former.

46. In Ex. 6 of the last chapter we saw how a melodic design of large compass could be divided among the different strings. A similiar procedure with wind instruments will be much less effective, because of the different qualities of their tones. As an example which cannot be considered satisfactory, we quote a passage by Hérold.

Here the effect of the scales in thirds is decidedly 'patchy,' because of the sudden changes in the quality of tone, and it is made still more conspicuous by the points at which the changes are made. It would have certainly been better here to have given the first

note of the second bar to the flutes, and to have introduced the
oboes at the second quaver—after, and not on, the accented note.

47. It must be understood that what has just been said as to
the dividing of passages between the wind does not apply to cases
in which one instrument repeats or echoes at a different pitch a
theme already announced by another.   Such a procedure is often
of excellent effect, as in the following :

Something similar will be found in Auber's ' Le Dieu et la
Bayadère' (p. 132 of the full score), where the theme is passed
along from one instrument to another, over sustained chords for
the strings.

48. It is seldom good, in solo passages, to double any wind
instrument *in unison*.   We are quite aware that this is not infrequently done, even by eminent composers.   A well-known and
striking example is the opening subject of the *allegro* of Schubert's
unfinished symphony in B minor, in which the melody is given to
one oboe and one clarinet in unison.   None the less, we consider
the effect in nearly every case more or less unsatisfactory ; and it
is not difficult to give the reason.   No two players produce *exactly*
the same quality of tone—probably not even if performing on the
same instrument.   The difference may be so small as to hardly
noticeable if each is playing singly, but the fact remains that two
flutes or oboes playing in unison do not give merely the effect of
a single one doubled in power ; there is also a difference in the
resultant quality.*

49. What has just been said about two instruments of the
same kind applies, even more strongly, to two instruments of

---

* The fact here stated is familiar to all who have had much experience in the
orchestra ; the author would suggest as a possible explanation (which, however,
he has had no opportunity of either verifying or disproving), that perhaps very
minute differences in the intonation of the two instruments—say, of a few vibrations only, which would pass unnoticed when each played alone, would set up
"beats" when the two played together, that would be sufficient to affect the
purity of the tone.

different kinds.   Each wind instrument has its own special quality
of tone, resulting (as the researches of Helmholtz have proved)
from the varying proportions in which the upper partial tones of
their tubes are present together with the fundamental tone.   When
two of these different qualities are combined in the unison, each
loses its purity, and the tone becomes turbid.   While entertaining
the very highest admiration for the genius of Schubert, we venture
to think that the opening of his B minor symphony, mentioned in
the last paragraph, would have been more effective had the melody
been given to the clarinet alone.

50. We are speaking now exclusively of *solo* passages.   For
tutti effects the unison of different instruments may often be used
with advantage, as in the following passage from the first finale of
' Euryanthe ' :

Here the subject is allotted to two flutes and two oboes in unison.
No single instrument would have given either the power or the
quality that Weber desired.

51. An excellent example of a melody played by the whole of the wood in unison and octaves is seen in the second movement of Tschaïkowsky's 'Symphonie Pathétique.'

Ex. 31. *Allegro con grazia.*   Tschaïkowsky : Symphonie Pathétique.

Notice here the charming effect of the counterpoint of the strings, *pizzicato*, in three octaves, against the melody of the wood. Observe also, as illustrating the balance of tone, of which we shall speak in a later chapter, how the horns and trumpets, which have simply subordinate parts, have to play *mp* and *p* against the *mf* of the other instruments.

52. Though the doubling of the wind in unison is seldom advisable in solo passages, many most beautiful effects are obtained by doubling them in the octave, or even in two octaves. Such effects are to be found in nearly every score; it will only be needful to give a few characteristic examples. Our first will be from Schubert's overture to 'Rosamunde.' *

* The piece commonly known as the overture to 'Rosamunde' was not composed for that work, but for the melodrama 'Die Zauberharfe.' The real overture to 'Rosamunde,' from which we quote here, was published as the overture to 'Alfonso und Estrella,' as it was performed at the beginning of that opera, for which Schubert wrote no overture.

(As in many other examples, we condense the string parts on two staves, to save space.)   We see here first, the flute and clarinet in octaves, and then the oboe and bassoon similarly treated.   In the last two bars, the bassoon is doubled also by the clarinet in unison —probably for the sake of getting the B♮ in the second crotchet, which Schubert was evidently afraid (as being too high) to write for the bassoon.   In modern music the note is frequently met with.

53. Of the possible combinations of two wind instruments in the octave, that of the flute and clarinet is one of the most frequently used. The blending of these two instruments is more perfect than that of any other two wind instruments, possibly because the flute, when playing the octave above the clarinet, supplies the partial-tone which is wanting in the latter instrument. (See Vol. I., § 284.) We give a short example by Weber.

The combinations of the flute and oboe, oboe and bassoon, and clarinet and bassoon in octaves, are also common; the oboe and clarinet, and the flute and bassoon are less frequently used in this way, though examples of both might be given, did space permit. A melody given to the wind in three octaves is also not uncommon; a good example will be seen in the Andante of Beethoven's symphony in C minor.

54. Our next illustration

shows the very effective use of arpeggios in the *chalumeau* of the clarinet, and is further interesting as being probably the earliest example of the employment of three timpani in the orchestra. It may be well to remind the student that ' Corni in B♭ ' always indicates the *lower* B flat. If the high B flat horns are required, they will be specially marked as 'in B♮ *alto*.'

55. The solemn march in the second act of Cherubini's 'Médée' opens with the following passage for wind instruments alone.

This being essentially a *tutti*, rather than a solo passage, there is nothing to be said against such doublings in the unison as are here seen.

56. The following extract from Beethoven's Mass in D

shows contrapuntal treatment of the wind instruments; it also exemplifies the doubling of different instruments in the unison and in the octave. Observe the sparing use made of the oboe, as further illustrating what was said in § 45.

57. Our next quotation

Ex. 37. *Presto.* Spohr: 2nd Symphony.

deserves careful examination. Here we see the trumpets and drums *piano* added to the wood-wind and horns.

58. It is by no means always necessary that a considerable number of instruments should be employed at once, as in some of the examples given above.   Very charming effects are often obtainable by *individualizing* the instruments, and letting them, so to speak, converse with one another.   In such cases, a very slight accompaniment is often quite sufficient, as in the following passage :

Ex. 38.

Here the flute, oboe, and clarinet imitate one another above a very simple harmony, first for horns and drums, and then for horns and bassoons. Notice especially the last three bars, with the passages in thirds repeated with different qualities of tone, and compare it with the unsatisfactory passage given in Ex. 28.

59. In our last example we have seen the alternation of single instruments; we now show how one group of wind instruments can answer another.

MOZART: Serenade in C minor.

In the eight bars of this passage we see four different groupings,—clarinets and horns, oboes and clarinets, horns and bassoons, and oboe, horns, and bassoons. At the last bar is seen the commencement of a new subject for the clarinet. For the order of the instruments, see what was said in § 38.

60. Our next example shows some new combinations.

The *pianissimo* of the brass, with which this passage begins, is an effect to which Schubert was very partial. Observe how, in the third and fourth bars the harmony of the trombones is completed by the bassoons; at bars 11 and 12 these instruments take the

upper, instead of the middle notes of the chords. The *legato* for
the trombones, seen in the third bar from the end, is only partially
possible. (Vol. I., § 443.)

61. The passage next to be given is somewhat curious.

Ex. 41.   Haydn: ' Passione.

It is unusual to find a single trombone, as here, combined with
the wood. Notice how many different varieties of tone Haydn
has obtained here within the limits of ten bars.

62. The following extract from Verdi's 'Requiem'

Ex. 42.

VERDI: 'Requiem.'

shows· the accompaniment of solo voices by wind instruments. Here the low notes of the first flute are below the clarinets. (Compare Ex. 26.) Observe also the effect of the holding low G for the horn, and the beautiful obbligato of the bassoon in the first two bars.

63. We next give an interesting and effective example of the doubling of all the parts of the harmony by instruments of different tone-colour.

Ex. 43.   *Andante.*   Schubert : Mass in E flat.

Oboe 1º.

Clarinetti in B.

Fagotti.

Tromboni 1, 2.

Trombone 3.

Here the upper part is played by the first oboe and first clarinet in unison, while the three lower parts of the harmony are given to the three trombones, which·are doubled respectively by the second clarinet and the two bassoons. The colouring here is very rich— one might almost say luscious.

64. The following passage

Ex. 44. *Allegro.*　　　　　　　AUBER: 'Le Domino Noir.'

shows nearly the entire mass of the wind instruments, first *piano*, then *forte*. The subject, given to the clarinets in thirds, is accompanied by the soft brass, with a curious shake for the oboe in the middle of the harmony. At the fifth bar the melody of the first clarinet is doubled by the piccolo, to give it more brightness. Note also the charming effect of the single notes for the kettledrums and the triangle alternately.

65. In our next example

Ex. 45.

we see the voice accompanied by *pianissimo* brass and timpani.

In the latter half of the passage the oboe doubles the voice in
the octave.   Observe that in the last two bars, the melody would
have been too high to be good for the first horn; the passage
is therefore continued by the trumpet, which, in its medium
register, can play *pianissimo* much more easily than the horn could
have done on its upper notes.

66. By increasing the number of his wind instruments, and by
including the cor anglais and the bass clarinet among the regular
constituents of his orchestra, Wagner has obtained some new
tone-colours.   As our next examples for this chapter, we select
two short passages from his scores.   The first is from the second
act of ' Lohengrin ' :—

Ex. 46.   *Moderato.*   WAGNER : ' Lohengrin.'

Flauti.

Cor Anglais.

Clarinetto 1.º
in B.

Clarinetto Basso
in B.

Fagotti.

Corno 2.do
in C.

ORTRUD.

In   fer - ner Ein-sam-keit des Wal - - des, wo

still   und friedsam ich ge - lebt,—

The student will remember that Wagner writes for the bass clarinet with the same transposition as for the ordinary clarinet (Vol. I., § 329); the part of the instrument will therefore sound a tone lower than it is written. A very peculiar effect is here obtained by giving the melody to the cor anglais and bass clarinet in octaves, and accompanying it by sustained chords, *pp*, for other wind instruments.

67. Our second illustration is more fully scored.

The first thing to be noticed here is the unusual order of the
instruments in the score. When speaking in the first volume
(Chapter II.) on this subject, we inadvertently omitted to mention
that Wagner in his later works sometimes departs from the usual
arrangement, apparently for the sake of getting the upper parts of
the harmony nearer together, and, similarly, the lower ones on
adjacent staves. This is what he has done here ; the cor anglais
is written not (as usual,) next to the oboe, but below the clarinet,
and, for a similar reason, the bassoons and the bass clarinet

which at the sixth bar have the bass of the harmony, are placed
below the horns.   This does not increase the difficulty of reading
the score, because Wagner indicates the instruments at the beginning of each line.   Note in the above passage how the melody
for the clarinet and horn in octaves is imitated by the oboe and
cor anglais in octaves, and then in the bass by the bass clarinet,
bassoons, and second horn, while other wind instruments sustain
the harmonies.   The whole passage is a beautiful piece of scoring,
which will repay close examination.

68. It will be seen that the greater part of this chapter consists
of illustrations.   This, from the nature of the subject, is almost
inevitable.   In the branches of orchestration to be treated in this
volume, it is impossible to lay down such hard and fast rules as
can be given for harmony or counterpoint.   No teacher can tell
a pupil that one particular combination of instruments is *right*,
and that another is *wrong*; any combination may be right in its
proper place.   For instance, one would hardly imagine that a
good combination could be made with the piccolo, bassoons,
double-basses, and big drum and cymbals, yet this is to be found
with the most excellent effect in Marcel's song " Piff, paff," in the
first act of ' Les Huguenots.'

Here the curious orchestration is admirably adapted to the dramatic situation, and to the fierce song of the old Huguenot soldier. There are probably many combinations, even of the instruments in ordinary use, which have never yet been tried, and the only way to teach the subject is by illustration. Let the student examine, not merely the passages quoted in this chapter, but all the scores he can get; his imagination (if he have any) will thereby be stimulated to invent effects for himself. By the help of the hints we shall give him in a later chapter of this volume on balance of tone, he will soon learn to judge for himself whether any combination that he puts on paper will be likely to sound effective, and even though he may, perhaps, never become a great colourist, he will at least be able to avoid serious mistakes.

CHAPTER IV.

THE SMALL ORCHESTRA.

69. By the "small orchestra," as already mentioned, is meant an orchestra consisting only of strings, wood-wind, and horns, without any other brass instruments, and with no instruments of percussion. Before proceeding further, it will be well to treat of this combination, for which many important works have been written, including a large number of fine symphonies by Haydn and Mozart; this will give us an opportunity of incidentally mentioning a number of points which could not be so appropriately dealt with elsewhere.

70. There is no mistake which students of orchestration are more apt to make than to imagine that to produce a great effect it is needful to use a large number of instruments. The scores of the great masters abound with proofs to the contrary. To say nothing of the symphonies of Haydn and Mozart, just referred to —one of which, Mozart's great symphony in G minor, is one of the most perfect masterpieces of musical literature—we may mention Mozart's 'Don Giovanni,' in which, excepting the overture and the two finales, only two numbers (the recitative " Don Ottavio, son morta," and the sextett in the second act) have any other accompaniment than that of the small orchestra. To quote more modern instances : in Mendelssohn's ' St. Paul,' out of 44 numbers, 28, or nearly two-thirds, have either no brass instruments at all, or only horns, while even in a work so full of orchestral colour as Berlioz's 'L'Enfance du Christ,' there is only one number in which trombones are employed, and trumpets are not found in the score at all. It is therefore quite possible to get plenty of effect and contrast from the small orchestra alone ; the effect of the full power of the orchestra is often so much the greater in proportion to the reserve with which it is employed.

71. The possible combinations of the strings, wood-wind, and horns are absolutely inexhaustible ; all that can be done here is, to select some characteristic passages illustrating some of the most frequent methods of treatment. But first it will be advisable to give an important general principle, which the student will do well carefully to observe. It is the following :—Each department of the orchestra—strings, wood, and brass, should make correct (though not necessarily complete) harmony by itself, independent of the other departments. If we examine the scores of the great

masters, we shall find that, though sometimes, perhaps from over-sight or inattention, this rule is disregarded, it is observed in the very large majority of cases.

72. It must be noticed that this rule cannot always apply to the natural horns and trumpets, owing to their incomplete scale. For example, in Mendelssohn's overture to the ' Midsum-mer Night's Dream' we find the following consecutive fifths between the trumpet and the ophicleide. (We quote only enough of the score to show the harmony.)

It is *possible* that Mendelssohn purposely introduced these very obtrusive fifths with dramatic intention ; but it seems more likely that, had he had valve-trumpets, he would have replaced the C in the second and third bars by A.

73. It should be added, in this connection, that the horns can be treated as belonging either to the group of the wood, or to that of the brass. The student has already learned (Vol. I., § 48) that these instruments are quite as frequently combined with the former as with the latter.

74. As an illustration of the point of which we are now speak-ing, let the student refer to Ex. 89 of Volume I. He will there see complete harmony for the wood, either with or without the horns, which also make correct harmony by themselves ; he will further notice that the harmony for the strings is also complete. In Ex. 94 of the same volume, which contains only one part for a wind instrument, the harmony for the strings is perfectly correct if the oboe be omitted. Many similar examples will be seen later in this volume.

75. When strings and wind are employed together in a *tutti*, the latter frequently double the former, either in the unison or in the octave. The following passage furnishes an example of this procedure.

Allegro non troppo.   AUBER: 'Les Diamans de la Couronne.'

Ex. 50.

Flauto.

Clarinetti in B.

Fagotti.

Corni in Eb.

Corni in Bb basso.

Viol. 1, 2.

Viola.

Cello e Basso.

In the latter half of this example it will be seen that the bassoons and horns sustain the notes which are given in arpeggio by the second violin and violoncello. This is a case of very frequent occurrence.

76. It is not always that the doubling is as exact as in our last quotation. In our next illustration

BEETHOVEN : ' King Stephen.'

Ex. 51.

it will be seen that the wind parts give a simplified form of the quaver passage, allotted to the violins.

77. In the following passage, taken from a beautiful, though little known concerto by Mozart,

Ex. 52. *Andante.*   Mozart : Piano Concerto in A, No. 12.

Oboi.

Corni in D.

Viol. 1.

Viol. 2.

Viola.

Bassi.

the wind parts are more independent.   Note first, in the first four
bars, the holding A in four octaves—an effect more common in
the works of older masters than in more modern scores.   Composers of the present day frequently seem to forget how much can
be done with a very few notes judiciously introduced.   The scores
of Haydn and Mozart are full of similar passages.   Observe also,
that in the last quaver of the fifth bar no ill effect results from the
collision of the C sharp on the viola with the D immediately
above it on the first horn, because of the different timbre of the
instruments.   Had both notes been given to strings, the effect
would have been harsher.   We shall meet with similar examples
later.

78. Our next example shows more independent treatment of
the wind.

BOIELDIEU : 'Le Nouveau Seigneur de Village.'

As bearing on what was said in § 70, it may be mentioned that the whole of the opera from which the above passage is taken— one of Boieldieu's most charming works—is scored for the small orchestra ; neither trumpets nor drums are used throughout the work.   In the original score of this passage, the first horn is in A, and the second in D ; to save space, we have written both on the same staff, transposing the first horn.

79. How much effect is obtainable from a very few instruments judiciously employed may be seen in the following :—

Here the melody of the celli is accompanied by the counterpoint of arpeggio quavers divided between the flute and clarinet.

80. The opening of the allegro of Bennett's overture to ' Die Waldnymphe' shows a melody for the first violins accompanied chiefly by iterated chords for the wind.

Ex. 55.   *Allegro ma con grazia.*   BENNETT : Overture, 'Die Waldnymphe.'

Clarinetti in B.

Fagotti.

Corni in F.

Viol. 1, 2.

Viola. Bassi.

81. In the examples hitherto given the wind parts have been mostly subordinate; we now give some in which they are of more importance. The first is the commencement of Rossini's air, " Di piacer mi balza il cor."

This passage, which will repay close examination, requires but few remarks. The solo for the first horn in the last four bars, though difficult, is by no means impracticable, as it contains few large skips, and is mostly written for the open notes of the instrument. Let the student notice how easy it is to read, and remember what was said in Vol. I., § 363.

82. Our next example shows a horn solo of a different kind.

Here a somewhat sombre colouring is obtained by the suppression of all the *acute* instruments of the orchestra. Let the student notice that here the general principle laid down in § 71 is disregarded in the third bar, though observed in the rest of the passage. No bad effect, however, results here, because of the affinity between the tone of the middle notes of the bassoons and that of the violas. The horn solo is written for the valve-horn, but it would be quite possible on the natural instrument.

83. To show how much variety is obtainable from similar combinations of instruments, we quote another passage, also without any acute instruments.

Ex. 58. MACKENZIE: 'La Belle Dame sans Merci.'

It would be difficult to find two passages more dissimilar in effect than our last example and this one; yet, excepting for the low notes of the second clarinet and the pizzicato of the double-basses, the instruments employed are the same in both. The rather thick effect of the chords low down in the bass was evidently intended by the composer.

84. The following extract from the overture to 'Semiramide'

shows a very pretty and elegant combination.   The sparkling
melody in the first violins is doubled in the upper octave by the
piccolo, and lightly accompanied by the other strings, with staccato chords for the horns.   Notice that the counterpoint in
arpeggio for the solo wind instruments is introduced, not against,
but between the semiquavers of the violins, and is therefore more
distinctly heard, and stands out with greater prominence.   These
few bars are a perfect model of neat and effective scoring.

85. Our next illustration is quite different from any yet seen
in this chapter.

Ex. 60.   *Nicht schnell.*   SCHUMANN : 3d Symphony.

We leave the student to analyze this beautiful passage for himself, merely remarking that in the first half the principal part is allotted to the wind, and in the second half to the strings. The horns here are obviously valve-horns.

86. We incidentally referred in § 77 to the treatment of passing notes. Unless very clumsily treated, they seldom produce any harsh effect ; * but it is frequently better that, if possible, the holding notes against which the passing notes form dissonances should be of a different quality of tone. An example by Haydn will illustrate this.

Ex. 61.   HAYDN : Symphony in G.   No. 58.

* In this respect the treatment of passing notes for the orchestra is much the as for the piano.

Though very simple in the means employed, this short passage is most effective. It should be noticed that the passing notes in the first violin seldom make dissonances in the same octave with the other strings, but only with the oboe and horn, the timbre of which is so different from that of the violins that no obscurity results.

87. An effect sometimes to be met with is that of two-part harmony, in which the upper part is given to the wind, and the lower to the strings. We give two examples, which are strongly contrasted with one another. Our first

BRAHMS : 2nd Symphony.

shows a passage *pianissimo* and legato ; the wind is in three
octaves, each part being played by a single instrument. The
strings are also in three octaves, as the double-bass plays with the
cello.   We have compressed the strings on two staves.

88. Our second example

is *forte* and staccato ; all the wood-wind and one horn are employed, and the subject for the wind is in four octaves. The strings are in three, as in the passage by Brahms.

89. The treatment of the *crescendo* is a matter of some importance. There are two ways in which this can be managed The same instruments may be employed throughout, all gradually increasing their power, or, beginning with only a few, new instru ments may be continually added. In the majority of cases, both methods are used. We give first an example of the former.

In this well-known passage, from the first movement of Beethoven's C minor symphony, no new instruments are added till the entry of the first flute at the third bar before the *fortissimo.* In the last bar of our quotation the trumpets (not shown here) enter. If the student will examine the score, he will see that, when in the recapitulation this passage is repeated, Beethoven employs the second method—that of introducing additional instruments in the course of the *crescendo.*

90. The following passage, from the trio in the first act of 'Les Deux Journées,' shows the combination of the two methods.

Ex. 65.

Cherubini : 'Les Deu Journées.'

Here it will be seen that, besides the *crescendo* in each part, new instruments enter in each bar—the second violins at the second bar, the oboes at the third, the flutes at the fourth, and the horns on the *forte*.

91. For a *diminuendo* the converse process will be employed, either with or without gradual reduction of the number of instruments used. A fine example will be seen at the end of the Funeral March in the Eroica symphony. We give as our illustration a less familiar passage—the close of the slow movement of Spohr's first symphony.

Ex. 66. *Larghetto con moto.* SPOHR: 1st Symphony, Op. 20.

The effect is here so clear that no explanation is necessary.

92. If the student has carefully examined and analyzed the numerous illustrations given in this chapter, he will be convinced of the correctness of the statement we made at the beginning of it, that abundance of variety and effect can be obtained from the small orchestra. Yet he must not suppose that the subject has been even approximately exhausted. Of the passages which we marked for quotation or reference before beginning to write the chapter, more than a dozen have not even been mentioned. It would be easier to write an entire volume on this branch of the subject alone than to condense what is of chief importance, as is here attempted, within the limits of a few pages. All that is possible is, to give a few characteristic examples, with such remarks as may be necessary to explain them. The subjects treated in the present volume are mostly such as can only be taught by example ; but the student should on no account restrict himself merely to the few passages here given. We recommend to him especially the study of the operas of Mozart ; * though now more than a century old, they are still perfect models of instrumentation, and the young composer will learn from them how much effect can be obtained from the small orchestra. If we have quoted but seldom from them in these volumes, it is only because they are so readily accessible that the student can easily procure them for himself.

---

* Full scores of ' Don Giovanni,' ' Figaro,' and ' Die Zaüberflöte are all published at reasonable prices in the Peters' edition.

CHAPTER V.

BALANCE OF TONE.

93. There are few matters which give more trouble to the student in his early attempts at orchestration than that of securing a proper balance of tone.   To a great extent this power can only be acquired by actual experience; yet there are some general principles which can be laid down for his guidance, and it is of these we shall speak in the present chapter.   Much can also be learned from the examination of the scores of the great composers; but such examination, to be really profitable, must be minute and intelligent, and careful notice must be taken of the relative strength of the various notes of the chords.

94. To secure a proper balance when writing for strings alone is generally not difficult ; for in a well-appointed orchestra the string parts will be approximately of the same strength.   It will mostly be sufficient in this case to attend to the position of the harmony—a question with which we have already dealt in Chapter II. of this volume.

95. In what has just been said, we are speaking of *tutti* effects, whether *forte* or *piano*.   But the term "balance of tone" means much more than this.   Very often, especially in modern music, the composer wishes one or two parts of the harmony to be more prominent than the rest ; in such a case, if he writes so that all the parts are of the same strength, he fails to secure the required balance.

96. To illustrate this point, let the student refer to a few of the examples given in Vol. I.   First look at the passage by Brahms given in Ex. 43.   Here the melody is given to the violoncelli, and, although all the parts are marked *piano*, sufficient prominence is obtained by the fact that these instruments are playing in their higher register (on the first string), while the violas are on their lower strings; and further, that the violins, which are above them, have only arpeggios, and not sustained melodies.

97. In the following example of the same volume (Ex. 44), the accompaniment to the melody is even lighter, and in the passage by Auber, seen in Ex. 46, the melody, given to the first violins and celli in unison, stands out with quite sufficient prominence, though the other string parts are doubled by bassoons and horns.

98. The question becomes considerably more complex when wind instruments are employed, either with or without the strings. In the first place no two kinds of wind instruments are of exactly the same strength. Speaking in general terms, it may be said that the flute is the weakest—except in its highest octave—and the clarinet the fullest in tone, of the wood-wind ; to which must be added the fact that, as we already know, each has its own distinctive quality, and these instruments do not blend in the same homogeneous way as the strings do. For example, we will take the chord of C major, in close position, for strings only.

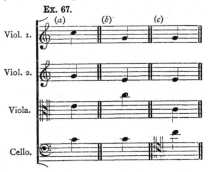

Ex. 67.

Here all the positions ,(a), (b), and (c) will be perfectly satisfactory in balance, though (c), with the melody on the cello, would only be used for a special effect.

99. Now let us write the same chord, in the same position, for four wood instruments of different quality.

Ex. 68.

We give only six, out of twenty-four possible arrangements of this chord ; but not one is wholly satisfactory, though for a particular effect any one of them might perhaps be employed. At (a) and (b) the weak C of the flute would not tell out enough against the reedy G of the oboe or bassoon below it. The chord at (c) would

sound rather better, as the G and E of the flute and clarinet will
blend fairly well, both with each other, and with the C of the
bassoon.   At (*d*) again, the flute is too weak, between the C of the
clarinet and the rather obtrusive low E of the oboe.   But no
chord will, in general, be entirely satisfactory where each note is
of a different tone-colour.*

100. A much better, as well as much more usual plan, in
writing four-part harmony for wind instruments, is to take two
pairs,—generally, either two oboes and two bassoons or two
clarinets and two bassoons.   The former of these combinations
has the more homogeneous quality, owing to the oboe and bassoon
being both double-reed instruments; the latter is the fuller and
richer in tone.   We give one short example of each.

Ex. 69. *Adagio molto.*   BEETHOVEN : 2nd Symphony.

Oboi.

Fagotti.

Ex. 70. *Presto assai.*   WEBER : 'Jubilee Overture.'

Clarinetti
in A.

Scherzando.

Fagotti.

101. Other, and less frequently used, combinations of pairs of
instruments will be seen in some of our preceding examples.   In
Ex. 101 of Vol. I. will be found two flutes and two oboes, and in
Ex. 39 of the present volume we have the combinations, first of
two clarinets and two horns, next of two oboes and two clarinets,
and, in the following bars, of two bassoons and two horns; while
in Ex. 40 we see at the fifth bar, two flutes and two clarinets.

* This statement must be accepted with a certain amount of reservation. As
we have often said, there is no rule in orchestral writing without its exceptions, and
we have already in this volume quoted two passages (Exs. 24, 25), which appear to
contradict what is here laid down.   But the student will see that those are both
written for solo instruments, and we are now speaking rather of the combination of
the orchestra *en masse.*

102. In the passage by Mozart just referred to, we see two horns combined with two wood-wind instruments. The student already knows that the horns are quite as often combined with the wood as with the other brass. It must not be forgotten that the round, mellow tone of the horn is more powerful than that of any single wood instrument, though it blends almost equally well with all. If, therefore, one of the middle parts of the harmony be allotted to it in a wind combination, that part will probably stand out with special distinctness. This point is illustrated in the first two bars of Ex. 36, where the first horn is in position intermediate between the clarinet and the bassoon.

103. A thoughtful examination of the numerous passages for wind instruments alone which were quoted in the third chapter will be of much value in aiding the student to judge of the proper balance between the different wind instruments; we must now proceed to speak of the combinations of the strings and wind which are met with in the " small orchestra " with which we dealt in the last chapter. The first thing to note is, that the relative power of strings and wind varies very greatly in different orchestras. In a small theatrical band, containing perhaps four first, and as many second violins, with other strings in proportion, the wood-wind would be far more prominent than in a large festival orchestra, in which there would probably be at least fifty strings. Sixteen first and sixteen second violins is by no means an unusual number in a modern orchestra; to balance this force would be required ten or twelve violas, and about the same number of violoncellos and double-basses. Against such a force as this the single wood-wind has much difficulty in making itself heard.*

104. The first point to notice regarding the combinations of the small orchestra is, that the tone of the strings in a mass is more powerful than that of the wood-wind, though with single instruments the converse is the case. For instance, one oboe or one clarinet is stronger than a single violin, but weaker than all the violins together; it is therefore necessary for the composer, if he wishes a single wind instrument to come into prominence, to be careful how he lays out the accompaniment to it. To refer to some of the solo passages quoted in Vol. I.—in Exs. 78, 81, and 82, we see solos for the flute accompanied by the strings. In

---

* The growth of the modern orchestra, while distinctly in the direction of increased sonority, is decidedly unfavourable to the performance of the works of the older masters, especially of Haydn and Mozart. It is known that Beethoven indicated an orchestra of from fifty to sixty as the proper number for the rendering of his symphonies; and it seems probable that even a smaller number was in general employed before his time. With our large modern orchestras, many of the solo effects in the works of the old masters are lost, especially if the music be of a polyphonic character. The most satisfactory rendering that the author ever heard of the fugued finale of Mozart's 'Jupiter' symphony was given by a small orchestra, containing eight first and six second violins, with four each of violas, celli, and double-basses. Against this small force, the important points of imitation for the solo wind instruments could be heard with the utmost distinctness. In the large orchestras of to-day, they are often lost altogether.

Ex. 78 the low notes of the flute are accompanied only by short pizzicato chords ; in Ex. 81 the flute is mostly employed in the upper register, the strings being sufficiently far below to obscure the melody in no degree ; while in Ex. 82, though all the violins in unison are accompanying the solo, the latter stands out with sufficient clearness, first because the violins have only detached semiquavers to play at some distance below the flute, and secondly, because they are marked *pianissimo* while the flute is only *piano*.

105. In the large majority of cases, the accompaniment to a solo should be (as in the examples just referred to) below, and not above it. If it be above, special care will be needed to obtain clearness. How this can be managed, the student may see by examining the accompaniment of the bassoon solo from ' Médée,' quoted in Ex. 110 of Vol. I. But it may be said in general that the only instrument that can make itself well heard *in the middle* of a mass of tone, whether of strings or of other wind, is the horn (we are, for the present, excluding the powerful trumpets and trombones, and speaking only of the small orchestra). In the following passage, from the Notturno of Mendelssohn's ' Midsummer Night's Dream ' music,

Ex. 71. *Con moto tranquillo.*   MENDELSSOHN : 'Midsummer Night's Dream.'

the solo for the first horn can be quite distinctly heard, in spite of all the parts that are above it. Had the passage been given to an oboe or clarinet with the same accompaniment it would have been difficult, if not impossible, to distinguish it.

106. More frequently, if the solo is in a middle part, it is given to a combination of instruments, instead of to one only. An excellent example of this is seen in the second subject of Mendelssohn's overture to 'The Hebrides.'

Ex. 72.

MENDELSSOHN : Overture, 'The Hebrides.'

Here, as the celli are marked *mf*, while the violins and violas are playing *pp*, the subject would have been quite clearly heard had no wind instruments been added to it ; as it is, it stands out, as Mendelssohn intended, with special prominence. A somewhat similiar passage will be seen in the same composer's overture to 'Ruy Blas.'

107. Mendelssohn's scores are such excellent models for the student that no apology is needed for making further quotations from his works. Two passages from the Adagio of the Scotch symphony furnish excellent illustrations of the point that we are now discussing—the treatment of a melody in a middle voice. We first give the opening theme of the movement, as it is at first presented, with the melody in the upper part.

Here the melody of the first violins is accompanied only by the light pizzicato of the other strings, and by sustained chords, *pp*, for clarinets and bassoons. When the subject recurs later in the movement, it is heard in the tenor, an octave lower than before.

Notice that here the pizzicato of the second violins and violas, and the holding notes for the wind, are nearly the same as before; but there are now two new counterpoints above the melody—the triplet semiquavers of the first violins, and the new subject (of which only the first notes are quoted) given by the flute and oboe in octaves. As these new upper parts would be likely to distract attention from, and to obscure the principal subject, the celli, to which the latter is given, are reinforced by the third horn.

108. The passage just quoted illustrates a very important point concerning polyphonic writing for the orchestra. As a general rule it may be said that, the larger the number of independent melodies, the more difficult it is to preserve clearness. In our last example this is done, partly by the contrasted rhythms of the first violin and the violoncello, and partly by the difference in colouring, the melody on the flute and oboe being of a quality of tone quite dissimilar to that of the strings to which the other subjects are allotted. In our next illustration,

E. PROUT: Suite de Ballet, Op. 28.

four different designs are seen in the orchestra, but the effect in
performance is perfectly clear. The chief subject is given, as in
Ex. 74, to the celli, here doubled in the octave by the first oboe ;
the *staccato* scale passages for the wood in the double octave
(piccolo and clarinet alternating with flute and bassoon,) are so
strongly contrasted with the chief theme that no confusion results,
even when the two themes cross one another ; while the background is furnished by the long shake, *pp*, for the first violins and
the pizzicato of the other strings. It is this marked difference in
the *timbre* of the various parts of the harmony that prevents the
effect being unsatisfactory.

109. We next give a passage illustrating balance from a
different point of view.

Ex. 76. *Allegretto quasi Andantino.*   GADE: 'Die Kreuzfahrer.'

Every bar of this quotation deserves to be carefully analyzed. Here we see an illustration of the effective combination in the unison of. wind instruments of different quality. (See §§ 50, 51.) In the first four bars the subject is given to the flute and oboe in unison; at the fifth bar, where the melody is not in the upper part, the second flute and second oboe, to which it is allotted, are reinforced by the first clarinet. Here is another example of what was said in § 106.

110. Observe further the arrangement of the wind in the opening bars. A single clarinet in its lower register would have been too weak against the two flutes and two oboes ; the part is therefore given to two clarinets in unison. On the other hand, the bassoons, if doubled by violoncellos, would have been too strong; a single instrument to each part is here quite enough. The harmony in the lower part of the orchestra should never be too thick.

111. One more point remains to be noticed. Look at the treatment of the dominant seventh in the last chord but one. For three bars the bassoons have been doubling the clarinets in the lower octave ; but here the second bassoon has A, not C, for the second crotchet. It would have been bad to double a seventh so low down in the harmony; the bassoon therefore takes A, the fifth of the chord, and, as the seventh would be too weak if given to the second clarinet only, this note is doubled in the unison by the second horn.

112. Some students may think such analysis as this needlessly minute, and ask, Why trouble ourselves about such small details as these? But the truth is, that it is precisely the attention to seemingly insignificant points of this kind that makes all the difference between well-balanced and ill-balanced scoring, and the more heed the student gives to such matters, the more satisfactory his orchestration will sound.

113. It was said in § 104 that in the small orchestra the mass of the wind was less powerful than that of the strings. A good illustration of this is seen in one of the very few miscalculated effects of orchestration to be found in the works of Beethoven.

Ex. 77.   *Molto vivace.*   Beethoven : 9th Symphony.

Flauti

Oboi.

Clarinetti in C.

Fagotti.

Corni in D.

Corni in B♭ basso.

Strings.

&c.

If, in this well-known passage, the strings play *fortissimo*, as in-dicated, it is quite impossible for the subject in the wood-wind to be clearly distinguished, while, if the strings play *mezzo-forte*, the whole character of the passage is changed. The incorrect balance of tone is due probably to the fact that the composer had been deaf for several years when he wrote the symphony.

114. Wagner, in his essay 'Zum Vortrag der neunten Sym-phonie Beethoven's' * (Gesammelte Schriften, Vol. IX. p. 277), suggests a re-scoring of the wind parts of this passage, so as to bring the melody into sufficient prominence. For this purpose he makes use of the valve-horns, which were unknown in Beet-hoven's time. Without committing ourselves to an approval of the principle of rescoring Beethoven, it must honestly be said that the effect in this case is greatly improved ; and the alteration is so instructive in its relation to the question of balance, which

* ' On the performance of Beethoven's ninth symphony.'

we are now discussing, as to make it worth while to quote the first bars, that the student may compare the two scores. He must remember that the flutes, and also the strings, are the same in both.

The student ought by this time to be able sufficiently to realize in his mind's ear the effect of a score, to see at once how far better the subject will be heard with this new disposition of the instruments.

115. It is not to be supposed, from what has been said above, that it is impossible to balance the wood against the strings ; Ex. 31 in the present volume shows the contrary. We now give another illustration which deserves close examination.

Ex. 79. *Andante moderato.*   BRAHMS: 'Ein Deutsches Requiem.'

Here we see three-part harmony. One part is given to the violins in octaves, a second to the wood with the horns in B flat, and a third to the remaining instruments of the score. The special point to be noticed is, that the wood, as here laid out, is not over-powered by the strings as it is in Ex. 77. Observe also that the trumpets are marked *f* and *mf*, while the other parts are *ff* and *f*.

116. Before proceeding to speak of the balance of tone of the full orchestra, we give one more illustration, showing how the wood-wind can be heard against the *fortissimo* of all the other instruments.

Ex. 80. Boieldieu: 'Jean de Paris.'

Notice here, first, that the piccolo is doubling the flute in the unison, instead of, as usual, in the upper octave. The two oboes and two clarinets bring out the melody in the middle octave with sufficient prominence to prevent its being overpowered by the strings and brass, especially as it is doubled in the upper octave by the two flutes, and in the lower by the two bassoons. The horns and trumpets of course play in octaves. But a very important point to be seen here is, that all the accompanying chords are *staccato*. Had the harmonies been sustained, the subject in the wind would have been nearly, if not quite, inaudible. Let the student also observe how carefully the "double stops" in the violin parts are written. They are all perfectly easy, and can be played in the first position. It will be instructive to compare this passage with that given in Ex. 77, and to notice why the effect is so much more satisfactory in the one case than in the other.

117. In a *tutti* passage for the full orchestra, the balance of tone is materially affected by the presence of the more powerful brass instruments—the trumpets and trombones, the tone of which, it must be remembered, is considerably stronger than that of the horns. Even if brass instruments are used alone, it is often the practice of composers to make the harmony complete on trumpets and trombones, and to use the horns merely for doubling, or filling up. Illustrations of this will be seen in some of the passages given in Vol. I. of this work. In Exs. 172 and 187 the horns are employed in this way.

118. A slightly different point is seen in Ex. 162 of the same volume. Here the first notes of the trumpets are accompanied by the trombones and tuba, of approximately equal power ; but, in the following triplets, the trumpet solo is accompanied by the less powerful tones of the four horns. In the third and fourth bars of this passage, where the horns are used to complete the harmony, two play in unison, to balance the tone of the trombones, which a single horn would scarcely have done.

119. The following passage gives a very good example of balance of tone for reed and brass instruments only.

Ex. 81. *Maestoso.*　　　　Rossini : 'Moïse.'

- gne ir renplit sa pro - messe,   Dans une saint-e   i - vres - se,

Viens re - ce - voir   sa   loi.

All these chords should be examined closely, to see the relative strength of the different notes.   When, as here and in some other French scores, the three trombones and ophicleide are all written on one staff, and there are only three notes, it is always understood that the ophicleide plays the bass in unison with the third trombone unless the contrary be said.　Reading the first chord upward, we see that the E in the bass is given to the third trombone and ophicleide and to the second bassoon.　The B above this is allotted to the second trombone and fourth horn ; the E (the octave of the bass) to the second trumpet and first bassoon ; the third of the chord, G♯, is heard on the first and third horns and on the first trombone ; while the upper note, B, is played by the two oboes, two clarinets, and the first trumpet.　In the following chords the upper B is stronger, being played by both trumpets; the reason probably being that when ' Moïse ' was produced (1827), only natural trumpets were used in the orchestra.　The student will see that there are no other notes of the harmony which would be natural notes for the trumpet in A.

120. At the end of our extract will be seen a roll for the drum on B, accompanying the chord of D major.　The effect is not very satisfactory (see Vol. I., § 480) ; but Rossini was very careless in this matter, and many passages could be quoted from his scores in which the drums have notes foreign to the harmony.　The student will do well not to imitate his example.

121. In the scores of the older masters, such as Haydn and Mozart, it is rare to find full harmony for the brass, such as that seen in our last example ; and the same is true of the large majority even of the works of Beethoven.　The reason is, that these scores seldom contained any parts for trombones ; in most cases, indeed, the only brass instruments employed were two horns and two trumpets, and these, being the old ' natural ' instruments, had only incomplete scales.　It was Weber who first introduced the trombones as regular constituents of the orchestra.

122. A very frequent method with the older composers was, to double the trumpets in the lower octave by the horns.　An instance of this is seen in the quotation from ' Jean de Paris ' (Ex. 80).　A more familiar example is furnished by the Andante of Beethoven's C minor symphony.

Ex. 82.　*Andante con moto.*　BEETHOVEN : 5th Symphony.

Oboi.

Corni e Trombe in C.

Timpani in C, G.

Viol 1, 2.

Viola.

Bassi.

The key of this movement (as most readers will remember) is A flat, but Beethoven has put both his horns and his trumpets into the key of C, for the sake of the energetic subject in that key which is here quoted, which occurs three times in the course of the movement. But the limitations to which the composer was subjected by the incomplete compass of the old brass instruments are well seen in another passage in the same movement—that in which a variation of the chief subject is heard in the basses of the orchestra. We give the passage in condensed score, as we are quoting it only to show the treatment of the trumpets.

Ex. 83.   BEETHOVEN : 5th Symphony.

Trombe in C.

Strings,
Wood, and
Horns.

Here the balance of tone is evidently disturbed by the abrupt cessation of the trumpets in the middle of a phrase; but the fault (if fault it be) rests, not with Beethoven, but with the imperfection of the instruments for which he had to write.

123. Another point of some importance is suggested by the examination of the above passage. It must be remembered that the brilliant tone of the trumpets will cause them to dominate the whole orchestra. The key of the music here is A flat, and in the tonic and dominant chords of that key, the notes C and G (the thirds of the respective chords) were the only ones which the the trumpet in C could give.* The octave G, in the last chord of our extract, gives undue prominence to the doubled leading note. This, as has just been said, was inevitable here, if the trumpets were to be used at all; but the effect would certainly have been better had they reinforced the dominant of the key, instead of the leading note. While it is impossible to lay down any absolute rule as to doubling in orchestral music, it will be found a good working rule for ordinary purposes to remember that the best notes to reinforce are generally the three chief notes of the key in which the music is—that is, the tonic, dominant, and subdominant.

124. When speaking in § 104 of the combinations of the small orchestra, it was said that the tone of the strings in a mass is more

---

* Excepting the B flat of the dominant chord, which is out of tune on the natural trumpet.

powerful than that of the wood-wind. If the full orchestra be employed, the wood sinks into a subordinate position, and is quite unable to assert itself. From overlooking this fact, Schubert, from whose scores we have quoted so many exquisite orchestral effects in this work, has made a very grave miscalculation in the peroration of the first movement of his great symphony in C.

SCHUBERT: Symphony in C, No. 7.

Ex. 84. *Allegro.*

Flauti. Oboi. Clarinetti.

Fagotti. Corni.

Trombe in C.

3 Tromboni.

Timpani in C, G.

Viol. 1, 2.

Bassi. (Viola col Basso all' 8ª)

Here the subject, which is, so to speak, the motto of the movement—being that which is heard at the commencement on the two horns in unison—is assigned to the wood and horns, and accompanied not only by the strings, but by trumpets, trombones, and drums. In spite of the '*ben marcato*' indicated for the wood, it is absolutely impossible for the principal subject to be heard with sufficient distinctness against the C, *fortissimo*, of all the strings, the trumpets and trombones. The fault is the same as in the passage from the Choral Symphony quoted in Ex. 77, but the balance, or rather the want of balance, is here even worse than in that passage. Had Schubert ever had the opportunity of hearing the symphony played, he would probably have rescored the whole of this peroration.*

125. In laying out a *tutti* for full orchestra, the student should first look to his string parts, and see that they are properly distributed. It must be noticed here, that it is possible, and even advisable at times, to separate the strings more widely than would be usual in other cases, and to fill up the intervals between them with the wind. An illustration of this will be seen presently (Ex. 86). Sometimes, as in a well-known passage near the close of the first movement of Beethoven's C minor symphony, only the outer parts of the harmony are given to the strings, and the middle parts are filled up by the wind ; but in the majority of cases the harmony of the strings will be complete.

126. The next thing to be attended to will be the brass ; for chords badly laid out for this department of the orchestra will ruin the effect of the combination. As a general rule, the harmony for the brass should not be in too close position ; the best result is mostly obtained by dispersing the harmony, approximately in the same way as one would treat voice parts. This principle applies alike, whether the brass be used alone (as in Exs. 172, 178 of Vol. I.), or whether it be combined with other instruments, as in the examples we are about to give. ·

127. If both strings and brass are suitably treated, it will be of comparatively secondary importance—in a *tutti*, be it always remembered—how the wood is placed, because in the large majority of cases they will be overpowered by the rest of the orchestra. They will generally be used for doubling some of the other parts, either in the unison or octave, though they are sometimes employed for long-holding notes against the moving harmony of other instruments.

* In performances of this symphony conductors frequently attempt to remedy the fault here spoken of by changing the *ff* of the strings and brass to *mf*; but even this is insufficient—to say nothing of the inartistic anticlimax produced by the sudden reduction of power in the orchestra just at the supreme moment. The best course would probably be to give the subject to the trombones in unison, as Wagner does at the end of the overture to ' Tannhäuser ' ; but the retouching of the scores of the great composers is objectionable on principle, and we must take them, as men take their wives, ' for better, for worse.'

128. We now give a few examples of different combinations of the full orchestra, illustrating some of the points just referred to. Our first is by Beethoven.

Ex. 85.
Maestoso.
BEETHOVEN: 'Christus am Oelberge.' ('Mount of Olives.')

In this and the two following examples we have written the
three trombones on one staff. It is more usual, and mostly
clearer, to write them on two. (See Vol. I., § 439.) In this
passage the tone obtained from the orchestra is full and rich,
rather than brilliant. This is because of the way in which the
second violin and viola parts are written ; it will be seen that they
are doubled by the brass, while the wood not only helps to
strengthen the rhythmic figure of the lower strings, but fills up
the harmony through nearly three octaves.

129. Our next example shows a more brilliant distribution of the orchestra.

Ex. 86. *Allegro molto.*   MENDELSSOHN: Overture, 'Ruy Blas.'

Here, to save space, we have put the four horns on the same staff; Mendelssohn's score contains parts for two horns in E flat and two in C. We have transposed the former pair, and the high B flat and G which are seen in the last bar of the horn part are the G and E of the E flat horns. Here the subject is given to the first and second violins in unison, doubled by the flutes, partly in the unison and partly in the octave above. The first oboe is in unison with the violins, while the second oboe and the two clarinets double them in the lower octave. The basses are doubled by the two bassoons, and the violas help to fill up the middle harmony, which by themselves they would obviously be quite insufficient to bring out with sufficient prominence. Mendelssohn therefore fills up his middle harmony with compact chords for the whole mass of the brass. It will be seen that in the second and fourth bars all the nine brass instruments lie within the compass of a major ninth. This appears to contradict what was said in § 126, as to the position of the chords for the brass; but the exception is justified by the fact that the upper melody is so strong that it needs a counterpoise lower down in the harmony. The close position, it will also be noticed, is only for a single bar at a time.

130. This passage, moreover, furnishes an illustration of what

was said in § 123 as to the best notes to double.   If these harmonies for the brass are closely examined, it will be noticed that
the notes to which the most strength is given are the tonic and
dominant of the key.   The trumpets—the most powerful and
brilliant of all the brass instruments—have no other notes than
these two.   That this was a matter of choice, and not of necessity,
is proved by the fact that later in the piece we find the complete
diatonic scale of C for the trumpets, showing that Mendelssohn
was writing, not for the natural, but for the valve instruments.
Similar treatment of the trumpets is seen in Ex. 85, and probably
for the same reason, because Beethoven, had he wished to bring
out the subject more prominently, could have doubled his first
and second trombones by the trumpets in the octave above.

131. After what has been said, our next example will need but
few remarks.

Ex. 87. *Allegro con fuoco.*
(Piccolo col Fl. 1.)   Rheinberger: 'Wallenstein.'

Here the violins, which play in thirds, are doubled in the unison
by the flutes (the first violin also by the piccolo in the octave),
and by the divided violas and clarinets in the octave below, while
the other wind instruments have massive chords.　The horn parts
illustrate a point that was incidentally touched on in § 118.　Look
especially at the third and fourth bars.　Here the horns are com-
pleting the harmony of the trombones, and each part is doubled,
in order to obtain a more perfect balance of tone.

132. It would be easy to multiply examples to any extent;

but it would be impossible to exhaust the subject, and the three passages we have quoted may be taken as fairly representative of some of the more usual methods adopted by composers. But if the examination of scores is to be of any real use to the student, it must not be merely superficial. He must try to reason out for himself *why* a passage is scored in a particular way. This is more especially the case as regards *tutti* passages. What we have endeavoured to do for him in the extracts we have examined in this chapter, he must try to do for himself in every score he studies, and when he tries writing a score himself, he must (especially at first) endeavour to calculate the effect, as regards balance, of every chord he puts on the paper. The more closely he has studied the scores of the great masters, the less likely he will be to make mistakes.

133. In concluding this chapter, it will be well to warn students against two important errors, into which beginners are very liable to fall, which are both connected with the questions which have been discussed in this chapter. The first is, a tendency to leave the middle of the harmony too thin. By this it is not meant that all the parts should necessarily be of the same strength. Often it is desirable that the outer parts should be the more prominent; but the middle of the orchestra should never be left too empty; to use a colloquial expression, the orchestra should not be "all top and bottom." If, in the passage from 'Ruy Blas' given in Ex. 86, all the brass be omitted, we shall see an illustration of this fault. By adding merely the horn parts, as they stand in the score, the balance would be to a considerable extent restored, though the *ensemble* would be far less brilliant than when the middle is filled up by all the brass.

134. The other mistake to be guarded against is the opposite of that to which we have just referred. Too great thickness in the middle of the orchestra should be carefully avoided. This sometimes results from the anxiety of the young composer to give every instrument something important to do ; but in the majority of cases it is caused by the injudicious position of the harmony. Except for special effects, such as that seen in Ex. 140 of Vol. I., close harmony should not be written low down, especially for the more powerful instruments. To understand our meaning, let the student turn to our last quotation (Ex. 87). In the first bar he will see thirds in the bass for the two bassoons. Here, in the *tutti* of the full orchestra, they do no harm ; but had the first and second trombones been playing in unison with the first bassoon, instead of an octave higher, we should have had an example of this objectionable thickness of which we are speaking. It is very seldom advisable to write chords in close position below the lowest G of the violins.

135. One piece of advice in conclusion. Let the student especially aim at *clearness* in his orchestration. We have already

incidentally referred to this point (§ 108), but it is of such great importance that it cannot be too strongly insisted upon.   One of the best ways to secure it is, to write mostly in not more than four or five real parts.   If there are more, the ear too often becomes bewildered in trying to unravel the tangled web of harmony.   The great composers mostly produce their effects by simple means.   Of course there are exceptions to this, as to nearly every other rule given in this work ; but if the student will examine all the examples in this volume, he will find that the large majority of them, when analyzed, will be found to be in four-, or at most five-part harmony.   Even in such passages as those in Exs. 18, 19, where the strings are divided into many parts, the doublings cause no loss of clearness, because the harmony is only in four parts.   If the harmony be pure, and the balance of the parts good, the student need be under no apprehension that his music will sound unclear.

CHAPTER VI.

CONTRAST AND COLOUR.

136. The subjects to be dealt with in the present chapter, while not among the most difficult to put in practice—at least for those who have any natural talent for orchestration—are by no means easy to teach, because the methods of obtaining contrast and the varieties of orchestral colouring are practically inexhaustible. We must remind students of what was said in the introduction to our first volume—that the use of the various colours supplied to us by the different instruments can only be taught to a limited extent. All that is possible is to offer a large selection of examples of various styles and schools, in order to stimulate the imagination of the young composer, and to add such explanatory and analytical remarks as will aid him to understand the general principles by which he should be guided.

137. If the scores of the middle of the last century, such as those of Bach, Handel, Graun, or Pergolesi, are compared with those of more recent composers, it will be seen that, while contrast was not unknown to the former,* it was with them rather the exception than the rule. The greater number of movements in their works are accompanied by the same combination of instruments throughout, generally by strings, with or without harpsichord. Obviously but little variety of colouring was possible under such circumstances. That which is actually found is largely produced by alternations of *piano* and *forte*.

138. With the modern orchestral resources, many ways of obtaining contrast are available—so many, in fact, that monotony is absolutely inexcusable. The different groups (strings, wood, and brass) may be employed alternately ; or the various members of one or more groups may be combined in almost innumerable ways. Even with the strings only, far more variety is possible than the student might imagine.

---

* It will be sufficient to remind students of such passages as the opening symphony in Handel's 'Dettingen Te Deum' or the Pastoral Symphony in Bach's 'Christmas Oratorio' to prove this.

139. To show this, it will be sufficient to refer to some of the passages for strings alone, given in Chapter II. of the present volume. In Ex. 1 we see a melody for the first violins contrasted with the arpeggios of the celli and the holding notes for second violins, violas, and double-basses. Ex. 3 shows still stronger contrasts, as pointed out in § 16. Let the student also examine Exs. 4, 7, 9, and 15, and observe the treatment of the separate parts of the harmony in each.

140. Contrast may be regarded in two aspects—the contrast of instruments employed *simultaneously*, or their contrast when employed *in succession*. All the examples referred to in our last paragraph belong to the former class. A similar example for wind instruments is seen in Ex. 23, where a flute solo is accompanied by soft chords for the brass. As illustrations of the contrast of instruments employed in succession, we will refer to Exs. 29 and 38; while Exs. 39, 40 show groups of instruments so treated.

141. It is impossible to lay down any fixed rule as to the frequency with which changes of colour should be made; the composer's taste and feeling will be his best guide. But it may perhaps be a fair general working rule that two consecutive musical periods should not be scored in exactly the same way. This recommendation is made with considerable diffidence, because many exceptions to it are to be found, even in the best models.

142. The exact point at which it is advisable to make a change of colour can be fixed with much less hesitation. It should always be *after* (and not immediately *before*) an accented note. In other words, the colouring should not be changed in the middle of a "motive" (*Musical Form*, § 69). It is largely owing to the disregard of this point, that the passage by Hérold given in Ex. 28 produces so unsatisfactory an effect.

143. The rule just given requires a little qualification, that its application may not be misunderstood. Let the student refer to Ex. 39 of this volume. Here the change of tone-colour is made in every case, excepting in the last bar, after an unaccented note. This is because nearly all the motives have "feminine endings" (*Musical Form*, § 28). The new motives begin on the fourth semiquaver of each bar, and the general principle laid down is only apparently, and not really, disregarded.

144. Look also at the next quotation (Ex. 40). Here it looks at first sight as if the rule were broken; but this is not really the case, because the second and third phrases begin with an accented note, and on the first beat of the bar. The important point to be noticed is, that the change is not made in either of these passages in the middle of a motive.

145. It need hardly be said that the rule does not apply to cases in which single chords in one department of the orchestra are imitated or repeated in another, as in the well-known passage

in the first movement of Beethoven's symphony in C minor, of
which we quote the commencement.

146. At the beginning of the finale of the 'Eroica' symphony,
the unison subject given by the strings, *pizzicato*, is echoed, note
by note, by the wind.

147. A somewhat analogous procedure, though quite different in effect, will be seen in the opening of the quintett in the first act of Auber's 'L'Ambassadrice.'

Ex. 90.   AUBER: 'L'Ambassadrice.'

Here we see contrast of colour not only in the melody, but in the accompaniment; there is also variety of rhythm.   The *pizzicato* of the lower strings against the sustained chords of horns and bassoons was a favourite combination with Auber (see Vol. I., Ex. 205), and produces an excellent effect.

148. We shall now give some examples of contrast, beginning with that between the different groups of instruments.   Our first illustration will be by Haydn, whose scores, though it is the fashion of the so-called "advanced school" to decry them as meagre and antiquated, are full of instruction for the student.

Ex. 91.   Haydn : Military Symphony.

Allegro.

Flauto.

Oboi.

Fagotto 1º

Strings.

&c.

The commencement of the first subject of the movement is here heard alternately on wood and strings.   Observe that in the first two bars the flute is below the oboes—in the first chord it has the bass of the harmony below the bassoon.   Haydn has here departed from the usual arrangement of the wind, evidently to obtain more contrast, and not to give the melody to the flute twice in succession.

149. Our next example—the opening bars of the magnificent introduction to the second act of Cherubini's 'Médée'—shows how much contrast and colour can be obtained by apparently the simplest means.

&c

The score looks almost like a row of empty staves; and yet how masterly the effect of a very few notes! Observe first the contrasts of rhythm; the staccato subject in the basses is answered by legato passages for the wood, while the violins maintain an agitated tremolo throughout. Note also the contrasts of *piano* and *forte*, and the effect of the *sforzando* chords of the horns, with the single stroke of the drum, at the end of each phrase. We must remark, by the way, that Cherubini has here, as in most of his earlier scores, written the clarinets as non-transposing instruments. The part would, of course, be played on B clarinets.

150. In the following passage

NICOLAI: 'Die lustigen Weiber von Windsor.'

other kinds of contrast are seen. The horn solo, unaccompanied, is answered by the upper strings in harmony ; in the third bar a short subject for oboe and clarinets is imitated by the strings ; while in the last two bars iterated chords are given to strings and wind alternately.

151. The seventh and eighth bars of the above passage illustrate what has been so often said in the course of this work—that there is hardly a rule of orchestration to which exceptions are not to be found. In § 142 we laid down the general principle that the tone-colour should not be changed in the middle of a motive. But in these bars the motives

are divided between the horns and oboes. The reason probably is that the passages, if written only for the horn, thus—

would have been difficult and uncertain, and the upper F♯ would have been too thin in tone to produce the *sforzando* effect required. The composer's judgment and experience must decide when such departures from the ordinary principles are advisable.

152. Our next illustration

Ex. 94.   Rossini: 'Le Comte Ory.'

shows a phrase for the first violins, answered by the wood in three octaves.   In the latter half we see the division of a phrase between the oboe and clarinet.   Notice the touch of colour imparted by the soft chords *staccato* for the four horns.

153. The opening symphony of the "Quis est homo" in Rossini's 'Stabat Mater' is a very beautiful example of contrasts between the strings and the wind.

This passage is so simple in construction as to require but few remarks.   The horns in low A are seldom to be met with, though those in low B flat are very common.   Observe how in the second bar the first bassoon gives the B, the bass of the harmony, a note not obtainable on the *natural* horn in A, for which Rossini wrote. The bassoon, whose tone amalgamates sufficiently well with the horn, is often used by the older composers to complete the harmony in this way.   The close of the extract is immediately followed by a *tutti* for full orchestra, *ff* and *staccato*, giving a further contrast to all that has preceded.

154. We now proceed to give examples of contrasts between the various wind instruments.   Our first illustration will be from one of Haydn's ' Salomon ' symphonies.

No remarks are needed here ; the passage is simplicity itself.

155. Among the great composers none has ever surpassed Schubert in the art of making the wind instruments, so to speak, converse with one another.   We give two exquisite examples, both from his music to ' Rosamunde.'

Ex. 97.   SCHUBERT : ' Rosamunde.'

Here is a charming dialogue between oboe and clarinet, other instruments joining in at the close of the passage.

156. The passage just given shows the contrast of two instruments employed simultaneously (§ 140); the following shows them
in succession.

Ex. 98.
Andantino.   SCHUBERT : 'Rosamunde.'

157. In the fourth movement of Raff's symphony, 'An das Vaterland,' the German national song, "Was ist des Deutschen Vaterland," is ingeniously divided among the different instruments.

Ex. 99.

Allegro dramatico.   RAFF: 1st Symphony.

The movement is in the key of G minor; but, as the entire passage here quoted is in C major, we have given it with that signature, so as to simplify the reading of the score by the omission of accidentals.

158. No composer ever understood the management of contrast and colour better than Auber; the fact that his scores are seldom to be met with will be sufficient justification for introducing in this chapter several examples from his pen. The first is a charming little passage from ‘Actéon’ :—

Notice here first the effect of the sustained A of the third and fourth horns against the *staccato* of all the other instruments. Note also, as an example of attention to apparently insignificant details, the change in the position of the last two chords: had they been the same as the first chord in the bar, the last notes of the clarinet solo would not have stood out so distinctly.

159. Our next example shows another kind of contrast.

Here the unison of the first four bars is answered by the full harmony of the following four. Observe the piquancy obtained by
giving the second phrase to the piccolo, and note the charming
effect here of the triangle (compare Vol. I., Ex. 205, which is also
by Auber).

160. A delightful little piece of scoring will be seen in the
following passage from the first act of 'Les Diamans de la Couronne':—

This extract beautifully illustrates the principle enunciated in § 142. It will be seen that the tone-colour is changed at the end of each two-bar section.

161. Our next examples are more modern. The first is by Wagner.

Ex. 103.

Mässig langsam.   WAGNER: 'Tristan und Isolde.'

Tod - - ge - weih - tes Haupt!...............

Tod - - ge - weih - tes Herz!

To save space, the string parts, which have a *forte* chord on the
first quaver of the passage and a tremolo, *pp*, in the last bar, are
omitted.   Here the contrast is between the reed instruments and
the *pianissimo* of the brass.   It is rendered still more striking by
the unexpected introduction of the chord of A major in the third
bar—Wagner's notation of the bass clarinet has been already referred to (§ 66).

162.   The last example of contrast now to be given,

Ex. 104.   TSCHAÏKOWSKY: 6th Symphony.
Allegro non troppo.

&c.

shows a somewhat unusual combination. The subject first announced in four-part harmony by divided violas and violoncellos
is repeated, with some modification, by two flutes and two clarinets.
It should be noticed that while the strings are mostly playing in
their medium and *higher* registers, the wind are chiefly in the
medium and *lower*.

163. By *Colour* is meant the particular quality of tone obtainable from the orchestra by any special combination of instruments.
Though varieties of colour are often used as a means of contrast,
as seen in many of the passages quoted in this chapter, the two
terms are not convertible. It is quite possible to get contrast
without colour, and colour without contrast. For instance, in
Ex. 2 of the present volume, there is contrast in the rhythmical
figures and phrasing of the various parts; but, all being for
strings, all have approximately the same colour. On the other
hand, in Ex. 48 of Vol. I., a most peculiar sombre colouring is
given to the orchestra by the employment of four violoncello
parts, all muted; but there is hardly any contrast.

164. It is quite impossible to give any fixed rules for colouring;
but a few general principles may be deduced from the practice of
the great composers, and illustrated by examples from their scores.
The first point to be noticed is, that a great effect in colour may
often be obtained by the simplest means, as in the following passage.

Ex. 105.

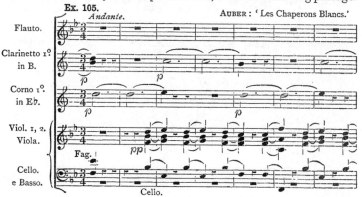

If the holding notes for clarinet and horn in the first part of this extract be omitted, the entire character is changed. Notice in the last four bars how the music takes a brighter tone by the doubling of the first violin by the flute in the octave above.

165. A very striking example of the effect of a single holding note is seen in the following illustration, from Verdi's 'Requiem.'

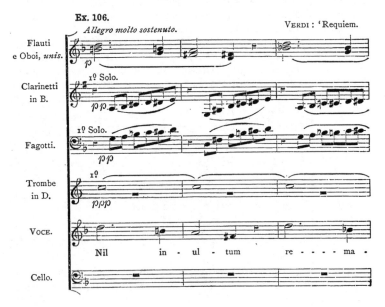

The trumpet is here *ppp*, while the other instruments are *p* and *pp*, yet the one note is heard most distinctly, and would be hardly less clearly distinguishable were it in the middle of the harmony, instead of the upper part. This passage also furnishes at the fourth bar a good example of the contrast of which we have been speaking in the earlier part of this chapter. Notice that the change of colour takes place after an accented note (§ 142).

166. If a bright, brilliant colour is required from the orchestra, the more acute instruments will predominate, and these will be frequently used in their higher register. In this case, however, care must be taken not to leave the middle of the harmony too thin (§ 133). The opening of the finale of Beethoven's C minor symphony, and the beginning of the third act of 'Lohengrin,' are good examples of scoring of this kind. But it is also possible

to obtain considerable brilliancy without employing the full orchestra. This will be seen in the following passage.

leggieramente.

The 'campanella' is a small bell, sounding the high F♯ shown in the score. Its entry alone in the second and fifth quavers gives much brightness to the passage. Observe that the wide interval between the first violin and the other strings is, so to speak, bridged over by the doubling of the melody in the lower octave, first by the oboe and then by the clarinet.

167. If, on the other hand, a sombre colour is wished, the higher instruments are sometimes altogether silent, and those which are used are employed chiefly in their lower or middle registers. Our next example illustrates this.

168. A very striking combination is seen in the following passage from Verdi's 'Requiem.'

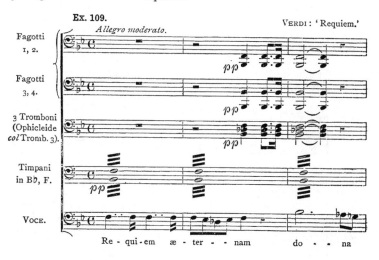

Ex. 109.   VERDI: 'Requiem.'

The double roll on two kettledrums is very unusual. It is performed by two players. The desolate effect in our example of the bare fifths accompanying the voice is very remarkable. Beethoven in the *adagio* of the ninth symphony also uses the two drums simultaneously; but the earliest instance we have found of a double roll is in Martini's opera 'Sapho,' produced at Paris in 1794.

169. Our next illustration—the opening symphony of the song " Glöcklein im Thale "—is a delightful piece of colouring, which will repay close examination.

Ex. 110.

Weber : ' Euryanthe.

170. We next give two specimens of religious colouring. The first is the commencement of the well-known air and chorus in ' Die Zauberflöte.'

Ex. 111.

Of Mozart's employment of the corno di bassetto in this scene we have already spoken (Vol. I., § 324). Here the solo and chorus of male voices is accompanied by soft chords for the trombones and the graver reed and stringed instruments. The violins and the double basses are silent.

171. Our other example, though its colour is entirely different from the preceding, is no less appropriate. It is a part of the opening symphony of the morning hymn of the Vestals, in the first act of Spontini's 'La Vestale.'

Ex. 112. *Larghetto con moto.*
SPONTINI : 'La Vestale.'

The solemn tones of the trombones, which Mozart employs in the Priests' music, would have been less suitable as an accompaniment to a chorus of maidens. Spontini therefore gives prominence to the tones of the flutes and clarinets. In the score the latter are written at their real pitch, as non-transposing instruments (Vol. I., § 304); we have written the parts for B clarinets, as they would certainly be played.

172. A beautiful little piece of colour, and as simple as it is beautiful, is the opening of the 'Shawl Dance' in the first act of Auber's 'Le Dieu et la Bayadère.'

Ex. 113.   *Andantino con moto.*   AUBER : 'Le Dieu et la Bayadère.'

Notice here the charming effect of the melody played by flute, clarinet, and harp, and the simplicity of the accompaniment. The score is a perfect picture.

173. Much variety of colour is often obtained by the *judicious* use of percussion instruments. We emphasize the word "judicious" because the beginner may be tempted to employ these instruments in season and out of season, and there is nothing which more readily vulgarizes a score than such a procedure. As good examples of the correct method we may refer to Exs. 191, 199, and 200 in our first volume. We now give a few more illustrations of this point.

174. Our first example

Ex. 114. *Tempo di Marcia.*   SPOHR: 'Fall of Babylon.'

shows a very felicitous employment of the side-drum, *pianissimo*, from the march of the Persian soldiers in Spohr's too-much neglected oratorio.   Note particularly the effect of the roll on the unaccented crotchets.

175. We next give a very fine piece of colouring from Verdi's ' Requiem.'

Here the sombre effect of the unisons, *pp*, for the strings is enhanced by the single note that follows—the low A of the double-basses *pizzicato*, and the soft stroke on the big drum.

176. The following passage is more curious.

Ex. 116. *Mouvement modéré de Valse.*   SAINT-SAËNS: ' Danse Macabre.'
Une cymbale frappée avec une baguette.

Cimbales.

Violino
Solo.

Viol. 1, 2.
Viola.

Bassi.

Saint-Saëns' 'Danse Macabre' is full of weird and strange experiments in colour. Here, instead of the cymbals being struck together in the usual way, a single cymbal is struck with a drumstick (Vol. I., § 520). The effect, when thus used, is somewhat similar to that of a gong, but less powerful, and the vibrations are not so prolonged.

177. Many novel effects of colouring are obtained from unusual combinations of instruments. Wagner, in his 'Ring des Nibelungen,' in which he employs three or four of each kind of wind instruments, has produced an almost endless number of new tints. We have only space to quote one here. Every one knows the effect of the low notes of the clarinets in the introduction of the overture to 'Der Freischütz.' Wagner, in 'Das Rheingold' and 'Götterdämmerung,' has gone farther in the same direction, by writing full harmony in four parts for three clarinets and bass clarinet. We give as our example of this effect the commencement of the dialogue between Alberich and Hagen in the first scene of the second act of 'Götterdämmerung.'

Ex. 117.
Lebhaft.   WAGNER: 'Götterdämmerung.'

3 Clarinetti
in B.

Clarinetto
Basso, in B.

Corno 4
in F.

Viola.

ALBERICH.

Schläfst du,   Ha - gen, mein Sohn?

Cello.

C. Basso.

This passage is not given for the student's imitation; it would be absurd for him to write for three clarinets and a bass clarinet;

but this chapter would be incomplete if it took no notice of the more recent developments of orchestration.

178. Among recently-produced works, Tschaïkowsky's 'Casse-noisette' Suite is particularly noteworthy for the ingenuity of its orchestral colouring. We select a few characteristic passages, which deserve careful attention from their great novelty of effect. They will also be found more than ordinarily useful practice in score-reading, less from any inherent complexity, than from the fact that it is more difficult for the student to realize fully in his mind the effect of a combination which he has presumably never heard, than to imagine the ordinary effects that are to be found in nearly every score.

179. Our first extract

shows a melody the first half of which is given to two flutes in unison, and the second half to the violins *pizzicato*. It must be remembered that the Glockenspiel sounds an octave higher than written, and is therefore in unison with the flutes, and not an octave below them. The extended arpeggios for the two clarinets, and the very low *staccato* notes for the bassoons, give a very singular accompaniment.

180. The next passage we shall quote is much simpler, but quite as original. Here a melody on the cor anglais is accompanied by *staccato* chords for three flutes.

Ex. 119.
Moderato assai.   TSCHAIKOWSKY : Suite, 'Casse-noisette.'

Flauti 1, 2.
Flauto 3.
Corno Inglese.
Clarinetto Basso, in B.

&c.

Notice the effect of the few notes for the bass clarinet at the end of the passage.

181. Our last quotation from this work is perhaps the most novel of the three.

Ex. 120.   *Andante non troppo.*   Tschaïkowsky: Suite, 'Casse-noisette.'

Here only a few of the strings are employed to accompanying the celesta,* an instrument of a very delicate tone. Had all been

* The *celesta* is an instrument invented some years ago by M. Mustel, of Paris. It has a keyboard like that of a piano, with a compass of four octaves, extending upwards from ⎘ . Its tone is produced by the striking with the hammers small steel bars, resembling tuning forks, and this tone, which is capable of considerable gradation, is delicate and ethereal, resembling that of very small bells. So far as we are aware, Tschaïkowsky's Suite is the only work in which it has been combined with the orchestra. In the score the composer directs that if the instrument is not available, the part is to be played on the piano.

used, the accompaniment would have been too strong.   The entry
of the bass clarinet is very curious ; it is indeed extremely difficult
to imagine the exact effect of the passage without having heard it.

182. The author trusts he will not be deemed unduly egotis-
tical if, for the last example, he gives a passage from his own pen.

Ex. 121.   E. PROUT : 'Alfred.'

Here a somewhat unusual effect is produced by the very low notes of the tuba doubling the bass in the chords of the reed instruments, which are answered by chords for horns, with constantly changing harmony.   For the colour required, no other instrument in the orchestra could replace the tuba here.   The nearest approach to it would have been the contrafagotto ; but this would have been too reedy, and it would have been almost impossible to subdue the tone sufficiently.

183. Though the examples in this chapter have been more than usually numerous, the author is painfully conscious, in concluding it, of the incomplete and inadequate way in which he has dealt with the subject—perhaps the most inexhaustible of all treated in this volume.   Only a comparatively small proportion of the passages he had noted have been given ; to treat the questions fully would require, not a chapter, but a volume.   At the risk of what Falstaff calls "damnable iteration," he must once more repeat the advice so often given to students in the present volume, to study the scores for themselves ; there is no other real way of learning.   It is hoped that the remarks here made on the examples quoted will assist the learner by showing him what to look for when studying alone, and by furnishing a few hints as to the direction that his researches should take.   If he has a natural feeling for colour, practice and experience will come to his aid ; and even if he have but little, his scoring, though it may not be picturesque, will, at all events, if he follows the principles illustrated by the works of the great masters, not sound ineffective.

CHAPTER VII.

THE COMBINATION OF THE ORGAN WITH THE ORCHESTRA.

184. Though, as was said in our first volume (§ 36), the organ is not a regular constituent of the orchestra, its employment in combination with other instruments can hardly be said to be infrequent.   Of late, at least in this country, the use of the orchestra in church services has become increasingly popular ; and, as the organ is never silent on such occasions, a few hints as to its suitable treatment under such circumstances may be usefully given in this place.   The mechanism, compass, &c., of the organ, so far as it is needful that the composer should be acquainted with them, have been already explained in Chapter XIII. of *Applied Forms.*

185. Berlioz, in his 'Instrumentation,' * says,

" It is doubtless possible to blend the organ with the divers constituent elements of the orchestra ; and it has even been many times done ; but it is strangely derogatory to this majestic instrument to reduce it to this secondary condition. . . . There seems to exist between these two powers a secret antipathy.   The Organ and the Orchestra are both Kings ; or rather, one is Emperor, the other, Pope ; their mission is not the same, their interests are too vast, and too diverse, to be confounded together."

186. Berlioz possessed so fine a feeling for orchestral combination and colouring that it is difficult to understand how he could have failed to see the many possibilities offered by the combination of the 'Emperor' and the 'Pope.'   The probable explanation may be that, at the time (1844) when his treatise was written, most of the scores in which the best examples are to be found were still unpublished ; it is at least certain that this was the case with many of them.

187. The earliest works in which we have found independent organ parts are those of Bach and Handel ; and even with these composers the parts were only written out in full when they were *obbligati.*   In other cases only a figured bass was given to be filled up by the player.   It is rather curious, when it is remembered how great an organist Bach was, that among his numerous concertos there is not one for the organ, though many movements with organ *obbligato* are to be found in his Church-cantatas.   As a specimen

* Page 127 of the English translation.

oɪ his polyphonic manner of treating the instrument when combined with the orchestra, we give a short passage from the 'Sinfonia' which opens the cantata "Geist und Seele wird verwirret."

Ex. 122.   J. S. BACH : Cantata, " Geist und Seele wird verwirret."

* *Taille* is the old French name for 'Tenor,' and is frequently used by Bach instead of 'Oboe da Caccia' (see Vol. I., § 250).

Here the organ simply adds one more part to the harmony.   It is
but seldom that, in such cases, Bach treats it in any other way.

188. With Handel the treatment of the organ as a solo instrument is, if we except the numerous organ concertos, much rarer
than with Bach.   Only three such examples are to be found in
the whole of his works.   We quote from the most interesting and
striking of these—the song, " But oh ! what art can teach ? " in the
Ode for St. Cecilia's Day, of which we give part of the opening
symphony.   It illustrates some points not shown in our last
extract.

Ex. 123.   HANDEL : Ode for St. Cecilia's Day.
Larghetto e mezzo piano.

ad lib.

It will be seen that Handel has here indicated the quality of tone that he wishes—the diapasons. In general the flue-stops of the organ blend with the orchestra much better than the reeds. The latter are mostly imitations, more or less successful—generally *less*—of the wind instruments, and when these are present, the reed-stops of the organ "pale their ineffectual fires." The flue-stops, on the other hand, add a new colour to the *ensemble*, and combine equally well with strings and wind.

189. To return to the passage before us; let the student observe how, in the first twelve bars, the orchestra is always introduced one crotchet later than the organ, thus allowing the solo instrument to assert itself. In the bars following the pause we see the organ answering the orchestra with charming effect.

190. As we are not writing a history of the combination of the organ with the orchestra,* we pass over, as requiring but few words, Handel's organ concertos. In these, such passages as that just given are rather rare; the organ is mostly treated in a florid style, and more often alternated than combined with the orchestra, which, with occasional exceptions, consists only of strings, doubled in the unison by oboes and bassoons.

191. The use of the organ in choruses will be referred to when we come to speak of the accompaniment of vocal music; we now proceed to give examples of its employment as a more or less prominent constituent of the orchestra. Our first illustration is the opening symphony of the "Et incarnatus" of Haydn's 4th Mass.

Ex. 124.   HAYDN: 4th Mass.

* Those who are interested in the matter may be referred to a series of articles on the subject by the author of the present volume, which appeared in *The Monthly Musical Record*, in March, April, and May, 1883.

Here the indication of the stop to be used, ' Flautino,' is a little
obscure.   The stop is of 4-feet pitch, and therefore would sound
an octave higher than written ; but it is difficult to believe that
this somewhat trivial effect is what the composer intended.   Probably a softly voiced flute stop was meant, and Haydn noted the
sounds as he wished them heard.*   The soft interludes of the
organ contrast charmingly with the melody given to the first violin
doubled by the bassoon in the lower octave.

192. Fifteen sonatas for organ with orchestra by Mozart are
published in the complete edition of his works, but in only five
of these is the organ part fully written out, and there is but little
in its treatment that is specially distinctive.   We prefer to quote
two excellent examples of the use of the organ from his sacred
music.   The first is the commencement of the air " Laudate
Dominum," in the first Vespers.

Ex. 125.   Mozart: 'Vesper de Dominica.'

* Perhaps the effect designed would be best reproduced either by playing the
organ part as written on a Stopped Diapason, or by playing it *an octave lower than
written* on a soft Flute of 4 feet.

Here the organ is chiefly used as a substitute for the wind instruments which are not in the score.

193. Our second example from Mozart is more curious.

Ex. 126. *Andante sostenuto.* MOZART: 15th Mass.

&c.

In this passage the organ is treated, in the right hand part, as if it were a solo wind instrument, and combined with the oboe and bassoon. In many of Mozart's works, written for small, or incomplete orchestras, we find one instrument doing duty in place of another that is missing. Here the organ solo looks as if it were a substitute for the clarinet, an instrument which was not in the orchestra at Salzburg, for which Mozart wrote most of his masses.

194. The next illustration we give shows the organ combined with brass instruments and harp.

Ex. 127. *Andante con moto.*   MENDELSSOHN : 98th Psalm.

Notice here, as bearing on the question of balance of tone, that the harp plays *forte*, while the organ and brass are *piano*. The effect of the combination is very fine.

195. Comparatively few modern scores are to be found in which the organ is used otherwise than as an accompaniment for voices. We now give a few examples of its treatment in concertos. An interesting work of this kind is Rheinberger's Concerto, Op. 137, for organ, with the accompaniment of strings and three horns. The variety of combination obtained with so few instruments is remarkable. We give two extracts.

In the first four bars of this passage the arpeggios of the organ
are accompanied by sustained chords for the horns; in the following bars the viola doubles the melody of the organ in the lower
octave, while the other strings play *pizzicato*; while in the last two
bars a good effect is obtained by the quavers for all the strings
forte against the sustained chords of the organ. It should be said
that in all cases the organ part is written in the original on three

staves ; in our quotations we compress it on two, to save space, where this can be done without the sacrifice of clearness.

196. In our other example from the same work

Ex. 129.

Con moto.

RHEINBERGER : Organ Concerto, Op. 137.

Corni 1, 2, in F.

Corno 3, in F.

Viol. 1.

Viol. 2.

Viola.

Bassi.

Organo.

the organ has chiefly accompaniment, the principal subject being divided between the violins and the horns. It is unusual to find the second horn part written so high as in the third and fifth bars of this passage (Vol. I., § 355). Rheinberger has in this work written the third horn below the second; in a performance it would be advisable for the second horn part to be played by the third horn, and *vice versâ*.

197. M. Guilmant, the celebrated French organist, has published, under the title of 'Symphony for organ and orchestra,' a work which is in reality an organ concerto, in which the full resources of the orchestra are brought into play, the score containing three trombones and tuba, and even (in the finale) the big drum and cymbals. Our first quotation from this work

Ex. 130. *Allegro.* GUILMANT: 1st Symphony for Organ and Orchestra.

is the beginning of the second subject of the first movement, and shows a quiet accompaniment for pizzicato strings to the flowing harmonies of the solo instrument.

198. In the following passage, taken from the same movement,

Ex. 131. *Allegro.*   Guilmant: 1st Symphony for Organ and Orchestra.

is seen the effective combination of the organ, *ff*, with nearly the whole orchestra.   No detailed analysis is needed.

199. In presenting several extracts from his own two organ concertos, the author's apology must be that they show combinations which he has been unable to find in any other scores that he has consulted. In the first to be given,

Ex. 132.

E. PROUT: 1st Organ Concerto.

the subject heard on the organ is imitated freely at a bar's distance by the violins. In the second half of the passage, the arpeggios of the organ accompany the themes given to the orchestra.

200. In our next example, taken from the coda of the Andante,

Ex. 133.   E. PROUT : 1st Organ Concerto.

the flowing subject in quavers for the organ is accompanied by a *pianissimo* roll for the timpani, and by fragments of the chief subject of the movement, given to the flute and horn in octaves.

201. Our last extract from this concerto

Ex. 134.   E. Prout : 1st Organ Concerto.

is the commencement of the choral "Gelobet seist du, Jesu Christ," which is introduced in the finale of the work. It is given out by four horns and one trombone in unison, against a florid counterpoint for the organ. Only the opening bars are quoted.

202. In the following passage

Ex. 135.   E. Prout : 2d Organ Concerto.

the melody is divided between the organ and the wind instruments, the latter being accompanied by pizzicato chords for the
strings.

203. In our final quotation,

Ex. 136.　　　　　　　　　　　E. PROUT: 2d Organ Concerto.

nothing but the melody is allotted to the organ, the entire harmony being given to the orchestra.

204. It will mostly be advisable for the composer, when combining the organ with the orchestra, to furnish some general indication as to the amount and kind of tone he desires. We have already spoken of the advisability of a very sparing employment of reed stops in such cases. In our last example, for instance, it would be absurd to play the organ part on a solo reed stop, such as the clarinet. The right quality here would be obtained by the use of soft 8 and 4 feet flute stops. But organs differ so much, that it is best not to go beyond general indications ; something must be left to the taste and judgment of the performer.

205. The organ is sometimes to be found in operatic scores. In such cases it is introduced in accordance with the requirements of the scene, and is seldom combined with the orchestra. It is either used as a solo instrument, as in the organ prelude introducing the prayer in the third act of Auber's ' Domino Noir,' or for the accompaniment of voices, as in the fifth act of ' Robert le Diable.'

206. In a few modern scores the HARMONIUM has been employed instead of the organ. From the nature of the instrument, its tone has but little carrying power ; neither can it adequately replace the organ. Its use is to support a chorus in passages of difficult or uncertain intonation. Liszt employs it in this way in his oratorio ' Christus,' and in the finale of his ' Dante ' symphony, in which he introduces a choir of female voices intoning the ' Magnificat.' Berlioz, in his ' Childhood of Christ,' accompanies the invisible chorus of angels, which ends the first part of the oratorio, with the harmonium. In each case the composer directs that the instrument shall be behind the orchestra. Excepting for such a purpose as this, the harmonium is of little use, and we know no instance of its employment in orchestral combination, properly so called, though, in some concerts, it is used to supply (which it does very imperfectly) the place of wind instruments.

CHAPTER VIII.

ORCHESTRAL ACCOMPANIMENT.

207. Hitherto we have treated of the orchestra as an independent force ; and, though a small proportion of the examples cited has had voice parts, the relation of the orchestra to the voice has been only incidentally touched on. But in vocal music, such as operas, oratorios, or cantatas, the orchestra in general takes a subordinate position, and becomes the medium of accompaniment. It is from this point of view that we have to deal with it in the present chapter. It will be convenient to divide our subject into two parts, and to speak first of the accompaniment of concertos and other instrumental solos, and then of the accompaniment of vocal music, whether for solo voices or for chorus.

208. Concertos have been written for nearly every instrument ; but by far the larger number existing are either for the piano or the violin. But, whatever instrument be selected, the general principles regulating the treatment of the orchestra in accompanying are the same. Of these, the first to be given, and one of the most important, is, *Always keep the orchestra subordinate to the solo instrument, excepting where the latter has merely the accompaniment.*

209. In order to accomplish this more effectually, it is mostly advisable with a large orchestra to let only a few desks of the strings accompany the soloist, the rest entering only in the interludes, &c., separating the different solo passages. In most modern concertos this is indicated by marking the different passages ' *Tutti* ' and ' *Solo*.' Where this has not been already done, the conductor should see to it. Exactly how many desks shall accompany the solos is a matter which must depend upon the size of the hall and other considerations ; no definite rule can be laid down.

210. Another important hint for the student is that it is desirable that the greater part of the accompaniments of a concerto should be allotted to the strings.   It must be understood that this by no means precludes the employment of the wind instruments, either alone or in combination with the strings, from time to time. But the same reasons given in our first volume (§§ 55–57) for the general predominance of the strings in orchestral writing apply with equal force here.   More especially is this the case with regard to their power of subduing their tone.   In very quiet solo passages, it is exceptional to find the accompaniment given to wind instruments.

211. The unobtrusive quality of the strings is another reason why they are so much used for accompaniment.   Their tone blends equally well with all instruments ; even in a violin concerto the soloist is always able to hold his own against them without difficulty ; for the tone of one violin differs essentially in *quality* from that of a number of violins playing in unison.*

212. With the conspicuous exception of Schubert, nearly all the great masters, and many who stand in the second rank, have written concertos for the piano.   In the earlier examples—in the concertos of Mozart and Dussek, for instance, the orchestral part, excepting in the *tuttis* which divide the different solos, is in general of quite secondary importance, though we find Mozart in his later works bringing the orchestra into more prominence, and foreshadowing the methods of procedure of Beethoven, whose piano concertos have been not inaptly described as " symphonies with piano *obbligato*."

213. Into the form of the concerto we do not enter here ; that has been already discussed in a preceding volume of this series.†   But there is one important difference between pianoforte concertos and those for all other instruments excepting the organ. In a concerto for a stringed or wind instrument the harmony has to be supplied by the orchestra ; it is rare, excepting in a cadenza, to find more than a very few bars left entirely without accompaniment.   Almost the only example of this that occurs to us is the

---

* This fact is perfectly well known to all who have much experience of orchestral concerts ; the probable explanation is that, with a number of instruments playing the same part, though each performer may play well in tune, there will be very slight differences of intonation—amounting possibly to only a few vibrations—not sufficient to be perceptibly false, yet enough to cause 'beats' when all are playing together.   It has been suggested that the peculiar resonance of a large mass of strings playing in unison is due to the presence of these beats.   Besides this, the slight differences in timbre of the individual instruments will render their combined tone different in quality from that of the soloist.

† *Applied Forms*, §§ 370–382, 478–483.

opening of Beethoven's Romance in G, Op. 40, for violin and orchestra.

Ex. 137.   BEETHOVEN : Violin Romance, Op. 40.

Here, it will be seen, the subject is announced by the solo violin in two-part harmony, and repeated in full harmony of four parts by the orchestra.

214. In a pianoforte concerto, on the other hand, one of the commonest effects is that of a dialogue between the solo instrument and the orchestra. An excellent example of this is found in the Rondo of Beethoven's great concerto in E flat, where the first subject, originally given to the piano alone, is divided—the phrases being alternately allotted to the piano and the full orchestra.

Ex. 138.   BEETHOVEN : Concerto in E flat, Op. 73.

Another striking example, though different in character and effect, will be seen in the slow movement of Beethoven's concerto in G.

215. Somewhat analogous is the following passage in which the cadence of each phrase for the piano is echoed by the strings.

Ex. 139.   GRIEG : Concerto, Op. 16.

216. More frequent than the alternation of piano and orchestra is their combination, the possible varieties of which are inexhaustible. We give a few illustrations of some of the more frequently used effects. In the first a *cantabile* melody is given to the piano, and accompanied by simple four-part harmony for the strings.

Ex. 140. *Larghetto.*   MOZART : Piano Concerto in D, No. 26.

In such a passage as this, it will be well not to write long notes in the upper part of the piano, as the tone is not very full, and has little sustaining power. A somewhat similar effect to the above will be seen near the end of the slow movement of Mendelssohn's concerto in G minor, where the subject is played in octaves by the piano, and accompanied by a *legato tremolo* for divided violins.

217. If an even lighter accompaniment to a melody than that shown in our last example is desired, the *pizzicato* of the strings may be employed.

&c.

218. The softer wind instruments may also be sometimes advantageously used for the purposes of accompaniment.

Observe here that the wind is marked *pp*, while the piano is *dolce*.

219. Very frequently the chief melody is in the orchestra, while the piano has ornamental figuration. An effective example of this is the following passage, from the first movement of Mendelssohn's G minor concerto.

Ex. 143. *Molto allegro con fuoco.*   MENDELSSOHN : Concerto in G minor.

220. Our next example shows two simultaneous melodies—one for the piano, and the other for the violins—accompanied by staccato chords for wind and strings alternately.

221. The examination of the numerous published scores of pianoforte concertos will show the student many other combinations, which we have not room here to quote. Before proceeding to speak of concertos for other instruments, we give, as our final example for the piano, a very novel and piquant passage from Liszt's first concerto.

Notice here the effect of the combination of the upper notes of the piano with the flute and triangle, while the harmony is supplied by the pizzicato of violins and viola.

222. In writing concertos for other instruments than the piano, the same general principles will be observed that have been illustrated in the examples that we have given. But besides the fact already referred to (§ 213), that other instruments require the orchestra to complete the harmony, it is necessary to remember that, in the case of a bowed instrument, the orchestra will produce a similar quality of tone ; and care must be taken so to lay out the score that the solo instrument is not obscured. Some of the many ways in which this can be effected will be shown in the extracts from various concertos that we shall now give.

223. In our first example, taken from the first movement of Beethoven's violin concerto,

Ex. 146. *Allegro ma non troppo.*   BEETHOVEN : Violin Concerto.

Oboi.

Clarinetti in A.

Fagotti.

Timpani in D. A.

Violino Principale.

the violin is accompanied only by reed instruments and drums. Here the contrast of tone between the solo instrument and the orchestra is very marked. Notice that at the end of the passage the real bass of the harmony is given to the drums.

224. In the following passage, taken from the Rondo of the same work,

Ex. 147.   Beethoven : Violin Concerto.

the subject is allotted to the bassoon, with a simple figure of accompaniment for the strings, while the solo instrument has a florid counterpoint in semiquavers. The passage has some analogy to that seen in Ex. 143.

225. In violin concertos much effect can be obtained by the soloist playing on the fourth string. (See Vol. I., § 61). An excellent illustration of this is found in the Adagio of Spohr's 'Scena Cantante.'

Here the *forte* of the solo instrument on the fourth string is distinctly heard through the other strings, though the first violins of the orchestra are in the second bar more than two octaves above the soloist.

226. Our next illustration

Ex. 149. *Allegro molto vivace.*   MENDELSSOHN : Violin Concerto.

shows a sustained melody for the solo violin, while fragments of the first subject of the movement are heard from the strings.

227. Our last quotation from a violin concerto illustrates a point that has not yet been mentioned.

Ex. 150. *Allegro energico.* BRUCH : Violin Concerto, Op. 26.

In a concerto many difficulties may be written for the soloist which no composer of judgment would think of writing for the orchestra. Such double-stops as those seen in the first part of this passage—especially in the third bar—would be altogether beyond the reach of average orchestral players. No doubt many men could be found in our best orchestras who could play them ; but it would be most unsafe to write them, for it is certain that many players could not be relied upon to do them justice. The passage here given is by no means the most difficult that could be quoted. To name but two modern works—Brahms' violin concerto and Joachim's Hungarian concerto are full of difficulties which tax the power of even the finest virtuosi.

228. Notice also in the above extract the contrast between the solo and the accompaniment, with its *sforzando* chords for the wind on the second crotchet of the bar, and the pizzicato full chords for the strings. Observe, too, how the chords are written, and compare what was said in Vol. I., §§ 78, 79.

229. It is comparatively seldom that solos with orchestral accompaniment are written for any other stringed instrument than the violin. The important solo part for the viola in Berlioz's ' Harold ' symphony is not a parallel case to those we are now considering, as this part is not written in the concerto style. Weber has written two solos for viola with orchestra ; and Schumann, Raff, and others have written concertos for the violoncello ; but both these instruments combine less well than the violin with the orchestra, owing to their lack of brilliancy ; and it is therefore difficult to make them effective.

230. Occasionally concertos have been written for more than one stringed instrument. A concerto in D minor, by J. S. Bach, for two violins is well known and frequently performed. Spohr has written two double concertos (or, as he calls them, ' Concertante'), Ops. 48 and 88, for two violins with orchestra, as well as a ' Quartett Concerto ' (Op. 131) for two violins, viola, and violoncello with orchestra. A very interesting work is Mozart's concerto in E flat, for violin and viola (see Vol. I., § 116), while Brahms has left us a double concerto for violin and violoncello.

231. If a concerto be written for a wind instrument, it will generally be best not to use another instrument of the same kind in the orchestra ; the only exception to this general principle being in the case of the horn, when the orchestral horn parts should be almost exclusively confined to the *tutti* passages. The

principle here enunciated is founded upon the practice of Mozart, in whose numerous concertos for wind instruments (flute, clarinet, bassoon, and horn) we find it invariably observed. It should be added that, if the solo part be for a wind instrument, the accompaniment should be chiefly for strings. If other wind instruments are employed, much care is needed, to preserve the due prominence of the solo part.

232. We have now to speak of the accompaniment of vocal music, and this naturally divides into two parts—the orchestration of solos, and that of choral music. We shall deal first with the former.

233. The simplest forms of orchestral accompaniment to vocal music are mostly to be found in recitatives. In older works, such as the oratorios of Handel or the operas of Mozart, we generally find what is known as "*recitativo secco*"—that is, a recitative accompanied only by a figured bass, the chords being filled up on the harpsichord, or piano.* Gluck in his later operas was, we believe, the first to accompany the recitatives throughout by the orchestra —with very rare exceptions, by strings only—and all modern composers follow this example. Except occasionally for a special effect (*e.g.*, in some of Marcel's recitatives in ' Les Huguenots '), the *recitativo secco* is quite obsolete.

234. As recitative is in reality declamation sung instead of spoken, and it is of the first importance that the words should be distinctly heard, the accompaniment should in general be very light, and wind instruments should either not be used at all—in the majority of cases they are not—or treated with extreme discretion. We recommend to the student a careful examination of the accompanied recitatives in ' Figaro ' (" Hai già vinta la causa," " E Susanna non vien," " Giunse alfin il momento "), in ' Don Giovanni ' (" Don Ottavio, son morta," " Crudele? ah, no, mio bene "), and in Mendelssohn's oratorios, as excellent models for the treatment of recitative.

235. Recitative is generally accompanied either by long-sustained harmonies for the strings, or by detached chords, the *tempo* being always free, and at the discretion of the singer. But very

---

* In England the custom prevailed until recently of filling up the harmonies by arpeggio chords on a violoncello ; and even now, though the employment of the piano has become much more general, the old and unwarrantable method is not wholly abandoned.

frequently interludes for the orchestra, in strict time, are introduced between the various phrases.   In such cases a fuller orchestration may be used, as there will be no fear of overpowering the voice.

236. As a fine illustration of what has just been said, we give a part of a recitative from Mendelssohn's ' St. Paul.'

Here the voice, with its declamatory passages, is accompanied
only by the *tremolo* of the second violins and violas, the singer
being left perfectly free; the incidental passages for the orchestra
are played in strict time. This quotation also furnishes a good
example of the combination of the organ with the orchestra, of
which we spoke in the last chapter.

237. It is not to be supposed that, even in the simpler recitative, the strings only are to be used for accompanying; the softer

wind instruments can also be very effectively employed in the
same way, as in the following passage :—

Ex. 152. *Adagio.* colla parte.   BEETHOVEN : Fidelio.'

Flauto.

Oboi.

Clarinetto 1º
in A.

Fagotto 1º

LEONORE.

So leuch-tet mir   ein   Far - ben - bo - gen, der

hell   auf   dun - keln Wol - ken   ruht,

Here the 'colla parte' indicates that strict time is not to be kept,
but that the instruments follow the singer. Beethoven probably
marked it because in his time the wind was rarely used in recitative as here.

238. Of the infinite variety of ways in which a vocal solo can
be accompanied it is impossible to mention more than a very few.
Several have been already seen in examples given in the preceding and in the present volume ; but, as the student will learn
more by an examination of good models than in any other way,
we shall give a few more illustrations, showing beautiful combinations of various kinds, and illustrating some points not yet touched
on. Our first quotation gives a simple melody, with a very light
accompaniment of *pizzicato* strings.

239. Another charming example of a light accompaniment for muted strings only is the commencement of Siegmund's " Liebes-lied " in the first act of ' Die Walküre.'

&c.

The shorter slurs here in the upper string parts indicate the phrasing, while the long slurs below show that two bars are to be played with the same bow. At the second and third quavers of the second bar will be seen consecutive seconds between the first violin and the voice. These are not objectionable here, because the violin part is only a broken chord, and the effect, as regards the harmonic progression, is the same as if F and E were sounded together, the D in the voice being only a passing note.*

* Compare *Applied Forms*, § 38.

240. Our next example shows more contrasts of colour.

Ex. 155.

men-ti, pie-tà, pie - tà di miei.... tor - men - ti.

A somewhat unusual effect is obtained here by the accompaniment of the voice by three-part harmony for the violoncelli in the
first four bars. In the rest of the passage is seen the alternation
of the divided celli with the wind instruments, while the violins'
pizzicato supply broken harmony.

241. A very charming effect is produced in the first act of
' La Dame Blanche' by the combination of a march-like rhythm
for the wind with *pizzicato* chords for the strings.

Ex. 156.   BOIELDIEU: 'La Dame Blanche.'

Allegro moderato.

Observe the quaint and characteristic staccato for the first bassoon.

242. In dramatic music the voices often become subordinate to the instruments. In the following passage, for instance,

SCHUBERT : 'Der vierjährige Posten.'

the singers have only ejaculations, while the melodies are allotted to the wind.

243. It is by no means unusual to find a voice accompanied by an *obbligato* instrument—either string or wind—sometimes throughout a whole movement; sometimes only for an incidental passage. As more or less familiar instances may be named the airs " Salve dimora " in Gounod's ' Faust,' and " Jours de mon enfance " in Hérold's ' Le Pré aux Clercs,' both with solo violin ; Annette's song in the third act of ' Der Freischütz,' with viola obbligato ; the cavatina, " Be thou faithful unto death," in Mendelssohn's ' St. Paul,' with violoncello ; and the song, " Parto, ma tu, ben mio," with clarinet obbligato, in Mozart's ' Clemenza di Tito.' We give as our illustration an incidental clarinet solo accompanying the soprano voice from Spohr's ' Jessonda.'

244. We next give a short passage showing the accompaniment of the voice by wind instruments only.

- - ven - ga   a con - so - - lar.

It is unusual to find the trombones placed, as here, under the voice. The explanation is, that the whole movement is accompanied only by wind. Rossini is often rather careless in writing for the trombones, which he always (at least, in all his scores which we have seen) writes on one staff. One can hardly imagine that the notes in the above extract are to be played by three trombones in unison; but the published score of 'Otello' gives no indication to the contrary. Similar doubtful cases are met with in some of his other operas.

245. In modern works brass instruments are sometimes used freely for the accompaniment of a solo voice. If this is done, great care is needed on the part of the composer not to overpower the singer. It is most important to remember that if the accompaniment be too loud, *the words become inaudible.* As excellent examples of a solo accompanied by brass may be named the bass solo "Mein Herr und Gott, nun ruf' ich dich," in the first act of 'Lohengrin,' and Mephistopheles' solo, "Voici des roses" in Berlioz's 'Faust.' It is worth noticing that the accompaniment of brass instruments is much more frequently used for a male than for a female voice.

246. In some cases it is possible to accompany a solo voice by the full orchestra without overpowering it. A very fine example of

this is to be found in the last act of 'Il Trovatore'; the passage is so interesting that it deserves careful examination.

Ex. 160. *Adagio.*   VERDI : 'Il Trovatore.'

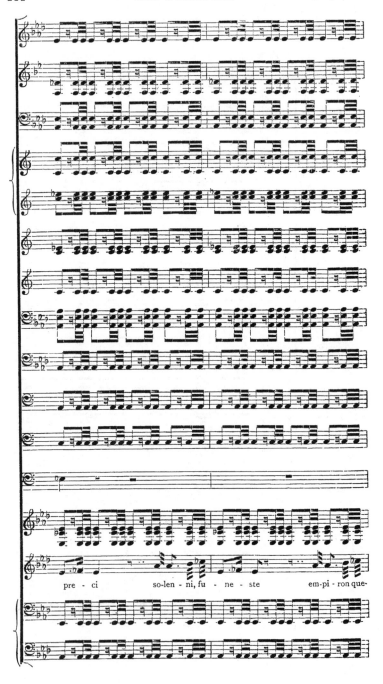

Here the voice, which is throughout in the medium, can be quite distinctly heard above the orchestra, though the latter includes no fewer than twelve brass instruments. This is effected partly by the rests in the orchestra, but still more by the fact that none of the instruments are above the voice, and all are playing *pianissimo* in their middle or lower registers.

247. If the whole orchestra is employed *forte* to accompany a solo, still more care is needed. In such cases it will often be advisable to let the full orchestra enter after or between, rather than with the singer. An excellent example of this procedure will be seen in Caspar's great song at the end of the first act of ' Der Freischütz,' while the close of the great scena, " Ocean, thou mighty monster," in ' Oberon,' in which Weber has been less careful about this point, is so heavily scored that it requires an exceptional voice to make head against the overpowering accompaniment.

248. The accompanying of choral music requires in general a different method of treatment from that adopted with solo voices. Here, also, consideration has to be taken of the size of the chorus, as compared with that of the orchestra. In a work written for a large choral society, numbering probably some hundreds of voices, a fuller and more powerful orchestration may be advisable than in accompanying an opera chorus, in which the voices will be hardly more numerous, and perhaps even fewer, than the orchestral players.*

249. The first principle to be laid down for the accompaniment of choral music is, that it is mostly desirable that the orchestra

---

* The present is the place to make a protest—in all probability unavailing—against the almost universal tendency (in this country, at least) to swamp the orchestra by too large a chorus. In the performance of modern works, this point is of less consequence, because they are mostly calculated for a very large choir, and scored accordingly. But in the works of the older masters, written for quite a different balance of power, a great deal of the effect is lost by the undue prominence of the voice parts in most choral performances. The late Hector Berlioz, than whom nobody ever more perfectly understood orchestral combination and the proper balance of power, gives in his treatise on ' Modern Instrumentation' (p. 241 of the English translation) his idea of the finest concert orchestra. It numbers in all 121 performers ; and he adds : " If a choral composition were to be executed, such an orchestra would require 46 sopranos (firsts and seconds), 40 tenors (firsts and seconds), 40 basses (first and seconds) "—a total of 126 voices. At the first performance of Verdi's ' Requiem,' in 1874, we learn from the published score that the orchestra numbered 110, and the chorus 120. Our English public—and probably the critics also—would no doubt raise an outcry that the orchestra was far too strong; but this is only because of the utterly false idea which generally prevails here as to the proper balance of orchestra and chorus.

should be employed in masses and groups, rather than for effects
of solo instruments.   Naturally, it is not meant by this that the
whole force should be continually at work—a tedious monotony
would be the result ; but breadth of effect, rather than minute
detail, should be aimed at.   This by no means excludes the pos-
sibility of giving prominence to orchestral figuration, when desired,
as in the following example by Haydn.

In this, as in the following examples, we have, to save space, written the voice parts in 'short score'; the student should, of course, in composing, give a separate staff to each voice. This passage illustrates what was said just now as to the balance of chorus and orchestra. The Mass from which it is taken was written for church use, and not for a large chorus; yet Haydn accompanies his voices not only by the orchestra, but by the organ, the use of which is indicated by the figured bass. An important melodic design, such as is here seen above the voices, will almost invariably be given to the strings. Wind instruments, even if several were playing in unison, would seldom be powerful enough to be distinctly heard above the chorus.

250. The above extract illustrates another point of some importance. In vocal music with a florid orchestral accompaniment, we frequently find strong dissonances caused by passing notes, similar to those already noted between different instruments (see §§ 77, 86). The difference of quality prevents any unpleasant effect, even when the dissonant notes are only a semitone apart, as in the third bar of the above, where the A of the soprano is sounded against the B flat of the violins.

251. Our next illustration shows a beautiful effect of a *pianissimo* chorus, accompanied first by a tremolo of strings, with holding notes for the bassoons, and afterwards by soft chords for horns and trombones.

Ex. 162. *Andante moderato.*   MOZART: 'Thamos.'

Fagotti.

Viol. 1, 2. Viola.

Soprano. Alto.

Den Gött - ern zu froh - - - - nen

Tenore. Basso.

Bassi.

sei un - - ser Be - stre - - - - ben. was

Notice in the last bar of this passage how the seventh of the
dominant chord, and the third of the tonic chord, both of which
are wanting in the voice parts, are given to the brass, to complete
the harmony.

252. In accompanying fugues, it will generally be best mostly
to double the voice parts in the unison and octave.   One of the
first essentials of effectiveness in fugal writing is perfect clearness,
and this will be best obtained by not overloading the accompaniment with detail.   It may be said against this view that we find
many fugues in Bach with independent counterpoints in the
orchestra; but the answer is, that it requires the almost miraculous
skill of Bach to treat so many real parts with freedom and effect.

253. Assuming, however, that the student has sufficient contrapuntal ability to write florid instrumental accompaniments to a
fugue, it will generally be best to write only one, or at most two,
moving parts.   An admirable example of this method of treatment
will be seen in the fugue "Behold now total darkness"—the
middle section of the chorus "Rise up, arise!" in Mendelssohn's
'St. Paul.'   He may also consult with advantage the various
examples given in Chapter XIII. of *Fugue*, and the final fugue
from Mendelssohn's 42nd Psalm, given in full on p. 202 of *Fugal
Analysis*.   But for the beginner, at any rate, it will be wise to
follow the advice given above, and to accompany a fugue chiefly,
if not entirely, in the unison and octave.

254. Great effect is often obtained by the unison of the full chorus accompanied by harmony in the orchestra. One short passage will suffice as an illustration.

Ex. 163.   MENDELSSOHN: 95th Psalm.

255. The converse case—the unison of the orchestra, accompanied by the chorus in harmony—is extremely rare. As an interesting curiosity we give, from the first finale of 'Oberon,' the only example of it that we can remember.

Ex. 164.   WEBER: 'Oberon.'

Now the evening watch is set

And from ev - ery min - a - ret   Soon the muez - zins call   to

256. In sacred music, the organ is often added to the orchestra for the accompaniment of choruses. With Bach and Handel, the instrument was used, almost or quite continuously, to double the voice parts. Modern composers more often (and with better effect) reserve it for the climaxes. We cannot afford space for examples, but would refer the student to the score of Beethoven's Mass in D (the first instance of a fully written out organ part—compare Ex. 161), to Mendelssohn's 'St. Paul' and 'Lobgesang,' and Gounod's Cecilian Mass.

257. For our final example, we give a beautiful passage accompanied by the full orchestra *piano*.

Ex. 165.   Rossini: 'Moïse.'

Observe especially the effect of the single chord *forte* of the brass and bassoons on the second quaver of the third bar.

258. It has been impossible in this chapter to deal fully with such an important subject as that here treated. All that could be done was to lay down a few general principles for the guidance of the student; the rest must be left to his judgment and musical feeling. Our last word of advice is, that, if he err at all in his accompaniment, it should be on the side of moderation, rather than of excess. The larger his acquaintance with the scores of the great masters, the less probability there will be of his making serious mistakes.

CHAPTER IX.

ARRANGING FOR THE ORCHESTRA.

259. It is very often desirable, and sometimes necessary, to arrange for the orchestra music written originally for the piano or organ. In many examinations this is one of the requirements; and although this volume is not designed in any way as a "cram" for candidates, yet, as the power of arranging music suitably for the orchestra may often be very useful, a few hints will be given in this chapter as to the chief points to be considered.

260. The mistake most commonly made by beginners in orchestral arrangement of pianoforte music is that of *keeping too close to the original.* On the piano the position of the harmony is often restricted by the impossibility of the hand stretching more than a certain interval—an octave, or at most a tenth; full chords are therefore often employed, especially by the older masters, low down on the keyboard. These do not on the piano produce a particularly bad effect, as the sounds begin to die away as soon as the notes have been struck; but if the chord were written in the same position for the orchestra, the effect would be hideous. As an illustration of what we mean, let us take the commencement of a sonata by Dussek; it is a passage which would be by no means unsuitable for orchestral arrangement.

Ex. 166. *Allegro vivace.*   Dussek : Sonata, Op. 13, No. 2.

Here it is quite clear that in the first three chords the composer
intends massive harmony ; but if only the exact notes here given
were written for the orchestra, it would sound nearly as bad as it
would be possible to make it. The chords for the left hand,
whether given to divided violoncellos or to bassoons, would be
horribly thick, and the middle of the harmony would be absolutely
empty.

261. For the guidance of the student, we now score these
bars.

We have scored the passage for the ordinary full orchestra of
Mozart and Beethoven.   In the third bar we have divided the
semiquaver figure between the first and second violins, to make
the passage rather easier.   In the second and third crotchets of
the fourth bar, the music would sound very empty, owing to the
distance between the bass and the upper part, had it been left as
Dussek wrote it.

262. It must not be supposed that the score just given is the
only good one possible for this passage : far from it.   If six ex-
perienced writers for the orchestra arranged the same piece, the
probability—almost the certainty—is that six different scores, all
good, would be the result.   Our example is simply intended to
show the student how to set to work.

263. In the passage just given no alteration of the text was
needed, except in the first three chords ; the rest merely required
filling up.   But considerably more modification will often be
necessary.   To illustrate this we take a few bars from one of
Beethoven's sonatas.

Ex. ᴉ 68.   Beethoven : Sonata, Op. 22.
Allegro con brio.

Here the left hand part, though *possible* for a very good violoncello player, would be as ineffective as it would be difficult.   The
first part of this passage would also be open to the same charge of
thinness, if transcribed literally, as the example from Dussek.

264. We now score this extract for a small orchestra ; the
character of the music requires neither trumpets nor drums.*

* Very foolish questions are sometimes set in examination papers.   In those of
a very popular and highly-esteemed examining body, which shall be nameless, we
have seen quiet passages from slow movements to be scored for "full orchestra,
employing . . . 4 horns, 2 trumpets, 3 trombones, and drums," where no composer with the least judgment would dream of using more than the small orchestra.
One of these absurdities is before us as we write.   Examiners should be more
thoughtful.

Ex. 169. *Allegro con brio.*

It would have been quite possible here to write an easy arpeggio
in semiquavers for the violoncello, similar to those on the second
violin and viola ; but quaver arpeggios will here be more effective.
It will be seen that the original figure is preserved, but in aug-
mentation.   The double basses could also take the arpeggios ;
but it is much better for them here to sound only the tonic—the
real bass of the harmony.

265. It will be seen that at the *crescendo* in the third bar the
first violins are doubled in unison by the two clarinets, and in the
octave by the first flute.   The indication ' 4ta Corda ' also gives
them a fuller tone, and helps to prevent the melody from being
obscured by the oboes above it.   No definite rules can be laid
down as to the amount of additional matter which it is judicious
to introduce ; this must be left to the judgment and experience of
the arranger.   The important point is, not to add what will obscure or deface the composer's original outline.   In the above
example this has been carefully attended to.

266. We now give another example, showing other points.   It
is the commencement of Schubert's song, " Gruppe aus dem
Tartarus."

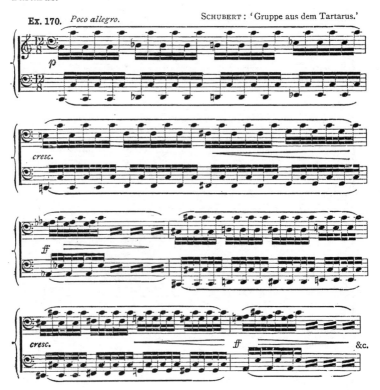

Ex. 170.   *Poco allegro.*   SCHUBERT : ' Gruppe aus dem Tartarus.'

This magnificent song, one of the most sombre and gloomy, almost terrific, in the whole domain of music, evidently requires quite a different tone-colour from the passages previously scored. The broken harmony amounts almost to a *tremolo*, and should be replaced on the orchestra by iterated notes for the strings. We now score these bars.

Ex. 171.

&c.

267. The *legato*, indicated by the slurs in the pianoforte part, is evidently impossible with the *tremolo* of the strings ; holding notes are therefore added for the wind.   The low sustained C for the two oboes will here produce an appropriately sinister effect. The brass is introduced at the *ff* to reinforce the volume of the tone ; strings and wood alone would be hardly sufficient here. No flutes are employed, as they would make the colour too bright. It will be seen that throughout the passage not a single note has been added to Schubert's original.

268. We now give another example, also from one of Schubert's songs, which we select as presenting considerably more difficulty in the way of effective arrangement than any of the passages we have yet scored, owing to the essentially pianoforte character of the figure of accompaniment.

Ex. 172.

By far the most suitable instrument to give this figure is certainly the harp; we shall therefore score the passage for harp, strings, and a few of the softer wind instruments.

269. The first thing to notice about this example is the addition in the first bars of chords for the wind.   It will be seen that Schubert indicates 'col Pedale' in the piano accompaniment. The student will hardly need to be reminded that the effect of this will be to sustain the harmony ; it was this indication that suggested the chords for the wind.   From the fourth bar, the first semiquaver on the harp is given to the left hand.   This is simply for technical reasons ; it is best on the harp to avoid (if possible) stretches exceeding an octave.

270. The distribution of the accompaniment among the various instruments is entirely at the discretion of the arranger; in the present case the points chiefly aimed at in the scoring have been clearness and contrast.   The example is not given as a perfect specimen, but merely as a model to show the student the general principles on which he should set to work.

271. If this passage had to be scored for an orchestra in which no harp was available, the difficulty of the arranger would be increased, but would be by no means insuperable.   Two possibilities would present themselves.   In the first place, the arpeggios might be begun by the flute, and continued by the clarinet.   We score a few bars on this plan, omitting the voice part.

These arpeggios on the clarinet would offer no technical difficulty, and would certainly be effective. But if the student will examine the song from which the passage is taken, he will see a practical objection to this method of scoring. It would be impossible, without ruining the effect, to change to another instrument in the middle of this passage; and, as it continues without a semiquaver's rest for more than forty bars, it would be too fatiguing for a wind instrument player. Considerations of this kind must never be overlooked. Were the passage only short, there would be nothing to say against the arrangement.

272. The other method of scoring this passage, and on the whole the best, if no harp were to be had, would be to divide the opening arpeggios between the upper strings, and to give the semiquavers, after the first two bars, to the violas. In this case, in order to secure a greater contrast of tone, it would be advisable to allot the figure which we have hitherto given to the violins, to wind instruments. The flutes would be best, for the tone of the oboes would be too incisive; while the passage, if given to clarinets, though quite practicable, lies too high to be in their most effective register. The upper C sharp, especially (which would be E on the A clarinet) would be rather "screamy." We score the opening bars in this way.

Ex. 175.

273. In selections from operas, fantasias, &c., it is often necessary to include the voice part or parts, as well as the accompaniment, in the orchestral arrangement. In such cases, care must be taken that the melody is rendered sufficiently prominent to be readily distinguished from its surroundings. In general it will be best to give the melody to a wind instrument—no other instrument of the same kind being used for the accompaniment. It may also be sometimes advisable to transpose a piece into a key more favourable for the solo instrument. To illustrate this, we will take the commencement of Schubert's song, 'Des Müller's Blumen':—

This lovely melody would be admirably suited for the horn. But, when treated as a solo instrument, the horn in F is almost invariably chosen; it would therefore be best to transpose the song into the key of B flat.

It will be seen that the melody now lies in the best and most expressive part of the horn's compass. It should be noticed that
the phrasing of the voice part is indicated for the horn ; it will
be well always to do this in making such an arrangement. Observe
also that as the accompaniment is so light, and lies entirely in the
tenor octave, only the graver stringed instruments are needed.
The quaver figure is given to the celli rather than to the violas,
because of the more expressive quality of the former. The celli
are divided, the seconds playing with the double-basses, as the
latter alone would be too far below the other instruments ; while
the sustained notes for the violas are added as a substitute for the
effect that would be obtained by the employment of the pedal on
the piano.

274. It is hoped that the examples we have given will have
sufficiently indicated to the student the general lines on which he
should proceed in arranging ; we now give a few examples of such
arrangements, as made by eminent composers. Our first will be
the interesting, though little known, arrangement by Beethoven of
his Funeral March from the Sonata, Op. 26. It was made in
1815, for the incidental music Beethoven wrote for the drama
'Leonore Prohaska.' The original is so familiar to every one that
it is needless to quote it. We first give the opening bars.

Ex. 178.   BEETHOVEN : ' Leonore Prohaska.'

It will be remembered that in the sonata this movement is in A
flat minor—one of the least favourable keys for the orchestra;
Beethoven has therefore transposed it.   It might have been ex-
pected that the transposition would have been either to G minor
or to A minor; possibly Beethoven selected B minor instead for
the sake of getting the low dominant on the kettle-drum.   In
either G or A, the dominant would have been one of the higher
notes of the drum, and the tone would have been less sombre and
funereal. Observe that the score contains no parts for the brighter
wind instruments—the oboes and trumpets. The subject is given
to the horns and bassoons, the harmony being doubled in the
upper octave by the flutes and clarinets.

275. We now quote the commencement of the trio in the
tonic major key.

Ex. 179.   BEETHOVEN: 'Leonore Prohaska.'

The scoring of the *tremolo* in the first two bars is analogous to that which was seen in Ex. 171. It will be profitable for the student to compare the fourth bar of this passage with the original. An *exact* transcription could not have been made effective on the orchestra.

276. A very interesting work, which the student will do well to examine, is Grieg's Suite, 'Aus Holberg's Zeit' (Op. 40). This was originally written as a pianoforte solo, and subsequently arranged by the composer for a stringed orchestra; a comparison of the two versions will show how much alteration may sometimes be necessary in orchestral transcription of pianoforte music.* We have only space to quote one passage.

* The work in both forms is published at a moderate price in the Peters' edition.

Ex. 180. *Allegro vivace.*   GRIEG: 'Aus Holberg's Zeit.'

The veriest beginner in orchestral writing will see at a glance that this passage needs very considerable alteration to make it effective or even practicable for the orchestra. We now give Grieg's arrangement for strings.

Ex. 181. *Allegro vivace.*   GRIEG: 'Aus Holberg's Zeit.'

After what has been already said in this chapter, no analysis of this passage will be required. The whole movement (Prelude) from which the above is taken will be found particularly instructive.

277. We must content ourselves with referring to many other examples of effective orchestral arrangement, which our limits forbid us to quote, and would recommend students to examine, if possible, the scores of Dvořák's ' Slavonic Dances,' and of Liszt's ' Hungarian Rhapsodies,' both originally written for the piano. Very interesting also is Mendelssohn's scoring of the accompaniment (originally written for the organ) of his anthem, ' Hear my prayer.'   Joachim's masterly arrangement of Schubert's great Duo in C, Op. 140—a work eminently orchestral in character— may also be strongly recommended.   For our final illustration we give a short passage from Berlioz's brilliant transcription for the orchestra of Weber's ' Invitation à la Valse,' as showing how a somewhat difficult passage can be divided between the different instruments.   We first give the original.

Ex. 182.   Weber: ' Invitation à la Valse.'

As D flat would be a dull key for the orchestra, Berlioz transposes
the piece into D major. The only other point to notice about
the score is the employment of the horns in three different keys.
This was done to obtain a larger number of open notes; at the
time this arrangement was made, valve-horns were not in general
use. (See Vol. I., § 362.)

Ex. 183. BERLIOZ-WEBER: 'Invitation à la Valse.

278. It has been impossible in this chapter, which deals with a very difficult subject, to do more than lay down some general principles for the guidance of the student. It is hoped that the numerous examples given may be of use to him ; but there is no branch of orchestration in which experience (and we may add *brains*) will be more needed than that of effectively arranging music not originally written for the orchestra.

CHAPTER X.

SCORING FOR INCOMPLETE ORCHESTRAS.

279. It will frequently happen that a composer will have either to write or arrange music for an orchestra in which some of the more important constituents are missing. This is more especially the case with local or provincial orchestras ; sometimes the necessary funds are wanting for engaging the full complement of performers ; at other times, more particularly in remote country districts, the players themselves are not to be had for love or money. In such cases it becomes necessary for the conductor to "cut his coat according to the cloth," and either to specially arrange the music for himself, or, if he be not competent to do this, to get somebody else who understands it to do it for him. The 'rough-and-ready' way adopted by some provincial societies of getting what instruments they can, and supplying all deficiencies by playing the accompaniment from a vocal score on a piano or organ, leads to results which are sometimes ludicrous, and always inartistic.

280. In the present chapter we purpose, therefore, to give a few hints for the guidance of those who may have occasion to score for an incomplete orchestra. It is obviously impossible to give rules that will meet all cases ; for while sometimes only a few of the comparatively less important instruments may be wanting, at other times there may be only three or four wind instruments in all.

281. The simplest case to deal with is that in which the orchestra contains only strings, and a work (either instrumental, or vocal with orchestral accompaniment,) has to be performed, which contains important parts for the wind. In this case, it would be best to have the wind parts played on a Mustel organ, or, failing that, on an American organ. The Mustel organ, owing to its greater expressive power, would be far the better, provided always that there is a player who knows how to manage the instrument. He should not be allowed to play from a vocal score ; but a special arrangement of the wind parts *only* should be made from the full score, unless the player be a sufficiently good musician to be able himself to fill up the parts at the instrument from a full score ; and it would be advisable to indicate the instrumentation in this arrangement, as far as possible, as a guide to the player in his choice of stops.

282. It will frequently happen, however, that, in addition to the strings, the orchestra may contain a few wind instruments. A not unlikely combination to be met with would be two flutes, one clarinet, one cornet (perhaps two), a trombone or euphonium, and possibly a pair of kettledrums. With such an orchestra as this, it is evident that no complete reproduction of the composer's effects could be obtained. It would still be necessary to fill up the missing parts on a harmonium or organ ; but the effect would, in any case, be more or less unsatisfactory.

283. If the orchestra were nearly complete, lacking only a few instruments, such, for instance, as the second oboe and bassoon, the third and fourth horns, and the trombones, it is most probable that, with a little rearrangement of the parts, the organ or harmonium could be dispensed with altogether—to the great advantage of the music, because the best imitative stops on these instruments sound poor by the side of the wind which they are supposed to represent. This brings us to a branch of our subject on which a few words must be said—the replacement of missing instruments by others.

284. It is principally in softer passages, written for only a few instruments, that the substitutions of which we have now to speak will be required. In *tuttis* there is almost always so much doubling of the parts that what is not heard on one instrument will most likely be played by another ; in any case, as each has its own part to play, it will seldom be advisable to make any change. But suppose a very common case—a duet for two wind instruments of the same kind (flutes, oboes, or clarinets) when there is only one in the orchestra. Then it becomes necessary to substitute for the missing instrument some other which shall approximate, as nearly as may be, to its tone. If, for example, there were a duet for flutes, and the orchestra had but one, it would be best to give the part for the second flute to a clarinet rather than to an oboe, as the reedy tone of the latter would mix much less well than would the clarinet with the clear and limpid notes of the flute. For instance, in Exs. 83, 84 of our first volume, a clarinet might be substituted for the second flute with very little loss of effect. Supposing, however, that the clarinets had also an important part at the same point, it might be necessary to give the second flute part to an oboe or even to a violin.

285. If it were a second oboe that was missing, and it had an important part, it would in general be better to replace it by a clarinet than by a flute, as the tone of the flute would be weak below that of the oboe. A second clarinet part would probably be more difficult to replace, owing to its extended compass. Its lower notes are not on either the flute or the oboe ; but the strong probability is, that if the orchestra contained only one clarinet, it would not have either a spare flute or oboe to make

good deficiencies. For a bassoon part a violoncello would be almost the only available substitute.

286. A very frequent case is that of an orchestra which contains but two horns having to play music in which there is an important part for four. In this case, the third and fourth horn parts can be taken by the bassoons, supposing the latter instruments to be disengaged at the time. The passage for four horns alone in the overture to 'Semiramide' (quoted in Ex. 152 of our first volume) could be very well managed in this way. For other brass instruments, owing to their powerful tone, no satisfactory substitutes can be suggested.

287. All the expedients we have mentioned are, at best, but mere makeshifts. We should strongly recommend those who have to select music for performance by incomplete orchestras to avoid, as far as possible, those modern works for which a very large orchestra is required, and more particularly those in which an important share of the work is allotted to the brass. It would be absurd to attempt to perform such pieces as the prelude to the third act of 'Lohengrin,' or Tschaïkowsky's 'Pathetic Symphony,' with a band containing not more than half-a-dozen wind instruments. There is so much good music arranged for small orchestra (overtures, operatic selections, &c.), that there is no necessity to mutilate music altogether beyond the reach of small bands.

288. Hitherto we have spoken only of the arrangement of orchestral music for a smaller force than that intended by the composer ; we must now say a few words about original composition for an incomplete orchestra. Here nothing is possible beyond a few general principles ; because hardly two incomplete orchestras will be exactly alike in their composition. Besides this, a composer, when writing for a special orchestra, is bound to consider not only what instruments he has, but what kind of players. In an amateur orchestra, for instance, it is more than possible that some at least of the wind instruments—perhaps even of the strings also—would be in the hands of very indifferent performers ; in such a case it would be worse than useless to write elaborate passages to which they could not possibly do justice.*

289. Very few examples are to be found in the works of the great masters of music written for incomplete orchestras, such as those of which we are now speaking. There are a few by Mozart, and one of great interest (of which we shall speak presently) by

---

* It may be interesting here for the author to give his own experience on this matter. His first *practical* acquaintance with orchestral writing was when, at the age of 18, he organized a small band among the boys at a school where he taught. The orchestra consisted of a few violins, one viola, one cello, *no* double-bass, two flutes, two flageolets, a piccolo, a cornet-à-piston, and a pair of kettledrums—probably one of the strangest combinations ever met with. Of course he had to score the whole of the music specially for this force. As the players were all beginners, the task was by no means easy ; but the experience acquired was of great value.

Wagner ; but the larger number of works with only a few wind instruments in the score contain just such (two oboes and two horns) as are among the least likely—at all events, in this country —to form the constituents of a small band.

290. It will, perhaps, seldom happen that an orchestra contains no violas ; but if this should be the case, it will be advisable, in order to obtain four-part harmony from the strings, to use double-stops for the second violin more freely than would otherwise be done. This, however, must depend to some extent on the players ; and, in any case, only such should be employed as can be easily played in the first position. As an illustration of this point, see Exs. 10 and 11 in our first volume. The effect of fuller harmony can also be obtained by giving to the second violin arpeggios and broken chords, similar to those seen in the first violin part of Ex. 33 of the present volume.

291. If there are only a few wood instruments, these should be chiefly used for solo effects, either for melodies (alone, or doubling the strings), or for independent counterpoints. The following passage, taken from one of Mozart's delightful minuets, will show both methods.

Ex. 184.   MOZART : 12 Menuetts : No. 5.

This passage also affords an excellent illustration of what was said in the last paragraph as to the treatment of the second violins when an orchestra contains no violas.

292. A few wind instruments can also be used effectively in combination, either with or without strings. A good instance of the employment of four instruments alone will be seen in Ex. 24 of the present volume. We now give a few bars for three wind instruments of different quality accompanied by *pizzicato* strings.

Most readers will remember this charming passage from the opening symphony of the song, " Deh vieni, non tardar." It admirably shows how beautiful an effect can be obtained with a very few instruments.

293. As the student may sometimes have to write for an orchestra with what is technically known as 'solo wind,' that is, only one of each kind of instrument, instead of the usual two, we give another example, again by Mozart.   It is from a little Contretanz : and, though hardly scored for the precise combination which is likely to be met with in small orchestras in this country, is useful as illustrating general principles.

Ex. 186.
Allegretto.   MOZART : Contretanz ('Der Sieg vom Helden Koburg'),

Note here first the independent counterpoint of the wood instruments to the melody played by the first violins, and, at the *piano* in the ninth bar, the charming effect of the subject for the wind, with the soft notes for the trumpets, and the filling up of the harmonies by the violins. If for the oboe we substitute a clarinet, and for the trumpet a cornet-à-piston, the effect will be equally satisfactory.

294. The treatment of the trumpet in this last example supplies a useful hint as to the management of the brass in a small orchestra. In all probability, the only brass instruments to be found in such will be one or two cornets, and possibly a euphonium. The student should be very careful in the treatment of the cornet. In our first volume (§ 417) it was pointed out that the tone of this instrument was devoid of nobility, and readily becomes coarse. Nothing is more calculated to give vulgarity to a piece of music than the allotting of important melodies to the cornet. This is more especially the case in a small orchestra, where the instrument is likely to be more prominent than in a larger one. It will therefore be generally best to restrict the cornet part to such holding notes and fillings up of the harmony as would be suitable for the horn or trumpet. In our last example, for instance, it would be far better to let the cornet play such a part as that which is here allotted to the trumpet, than to let it double the first violin in the lower octave, which it could do with the greatest ease.

295. One of the most interesting scores for an incomplete orchestra is that of Wagner's 'Siegfried Idyll.' In addition to the strings, there are parts for one flute, one oboe, two clarinets, one bassoon, two horns, and one trumpet; and with this small force Wagner has produced some very charming effects. A few short extracts from the score will conclude this chapter.

Ex. 187. *Ruhig bewegt.*   WAGNER: 'Siegfried Idyll.'

1 Oboe.

2 Clarinetti in A.

1 Fagotto.

2 Corni in E.

Viol. 2.

Viola.

Cello e Basso.

296. This passage furnishes an instance of the devices to which the composer must have recourse in writing for a few instruments. Had Wagner been scoring this passage for the ordinary orchestra, there can be little doubt that he would have given the duet passages for the wind here seen to two instruments of the same kind—probably the first to two oboes, the second either

to two clarinets or to two horns, and the third to two bassoons. The student will get a hint from this passage how to arrange a few instruments in similar cases.

297. Our next quotation, taken from the middle movement of the same work, is simpler.

Here is four-part harmony for the wind, which, with an ordinary orchestra, Wagner would probably have scored for two clarinets and two bassoons. The melody is here given not to the flute, but to the clarinet (compare the passage from Liszt's Concerto in A, quoted in Ex. 26). It is doubtless the superior expressive power of the clarinet that here decided Wagner's choice ; on the flute the passage would have been much tamer.

298. Our last example, taken from the same movement, is fuller.

Here the chief idea of the first movement, which we have already seen in the second violin part of Ex. 187, is combined with a modified form of the melody of our last quotation ; the bass of the passage is given to the bassoon, reinforced on its accented notes by the *pizzicato* of the double-basses ; while the second violins and violas have the middle parts of the harmony. We recommend the student, if he have the opportunity, to study carefully the score of the 'Siegfried Idyll'; he will learn much that will be of service to him if he should have to write for a small band.

299. Nothing is more impossible than to deal exhaustively with the subject we have been discussing in this chapter. It requires, perhaps, even more experience and tact to score for a very incomplete orchestra than for a very full one. But the same general principles must guide the student in both cases. Especial attention must be paid to the position of the harmony, and the balance of tone, rules for which were given in the fifth chapter of this volume. Once more it must be repeated that this cannot be learned entirely from any book. But the student may get many ideas on the subject by listening attentively to the performances of small bands, such as are often to be heard at theatres. Even from a badly balanced orchestra, with badly arranged music, he may learn what to avoid. His own artistic perception and judgment must do the rest for him.

CHAPTER XI.

CHAMBER MUSIC.

300. Though, strictly speaking, chamber music cannot be considered as a department of orchestral music, it has been impossible to deal with the subject in any of the earlier volumes of this series, because, excepting the piano, the technique of the various instruments employed had not been explained. The present chapter may therefore be regarded as an appendix to, rather than an integral part of this volume.

301. In its proper sense, chamber music would mean all music written for home use, and for private performance, as distinguished from that intended for concert purposes. This would include, not only the class of works of which we are going to speak, but the large majority of pianoforte solos, and songs with piano accompaniment. But the term has come to have a conventional meaning; and, as a matter of fact, chamber music is heard nearly, if not quite, as often in public as in private.

302. By CHAMBER MUSIC is understood music composed for two or more solo instruments. If, as happens in the large majority of cases, some (if not all) of these should be stringed instruments, the parts are never intended to be played, as in orchestral music, by several instruments each. This is sometimes done at concerts;* but it is a vandalism against which an emphatic protest should be entered.

303. Chamber music may be broadly divided into two kinds:—that without, and that with the piano. Before we proceed to speak of each of these separately, it will be well to give a few general principles, which apply equally to both. First, as regards the *form* in which chamber music should be written. If we examine the almost innumerable specimens left us by the great composers, we find that, in the overwhelming majority of them, one of the large cyclic forms (*Applied Forms*, chap. xii.) is used—generally the same form as that adopted for sonatas and symphonies. The reason, no doubt, is, that this form offers a larger amount of variety, and places more resources at the disposal of the composer than any other. The Suite form has also occasionally

---

* Haydn's Variations on the Austrian National Hymn, from his Quartett in C, Op. 76, No. 3, and Schubert's Variations from his Quartett in D minor, have been played in this way at the Crystal Palace, by all the strings of the orchestra; and Schumann's Quintett was similarly performed some time since, at the Conservatoire Concerts in Paris.

been employed by modern writers ; and some few have experimented in other directions. These are, however, rare exceptions, and they are not recommended for imitation.

304. The older composers sometimes selected the two-movement form ; several of Mozart's sonatas for piano and violin have only two movements. But, from the time of Beethoven* onwards, the three- and four-movement forms have been almost, if not quite, universally adopted, the former being seldom met with when more than two instruments are employed, though it is by no means uncommon in sonatas written for piano and violin, or violoncello.

305. Occasionally, instead of complete cyclic forms, we meet with single movements written for more than one instrument. Mozart has left two sets of variations for piano and violin, Beethoven a rondo and a set of variations for the same instruments, besides some variations for piano and violoncello, and two sets (Ops. 44 and 121) for piano, violin, and violoncello. Among many other instances that might be given, it will suffice to name Schubert's Rondo in B minor, Op. 70, for piano and violin, and Chopin's Polonaise in C, Op. 3, for piano and violoncello.

306. A very important distinction between chamber and orchestral music is, that, whereas in the latter, some of the parts (*e.g.*, the second violin and viola, and the second wind instruments) will generally occupy a comparatively subordinate position, in chamber music all should be, as nearly as possible, of equal importance. A well-written quartett or trio, whether for strings alone, or with piano, should be, so to speak, a living organism, each instrument having its own important part to contribute to the general effect. If any one instrument is either too prominent, or unduly subordinate, the artistic unity of the work will inevitably suffer. To illustrate this, let the student compare one of Haydn's pianoforte trios with one by Beethoven, Schubert, or Mendelssohn. In Haydn's trios, the part for the violoncello is comparatively so unimportant (frequently merely doubling the bass of the piano) that in many passages it could be omitted without serious injury to the music. † But in the later examples to which we have referred, the part of the violoncello is in no degree subordinate to that of the piano or violin. The difference in the treatment may perhaps explain to some extent the neglect of Haydn's otherwise very charming trios. " If one member suffer, all the others suffer with it."

---

* Beethoven's two Sonatas, Op. 5, for piano and violoncello, are the only exceptions ; and in both of these, the introductory Adagio, though leading directly into the following Allegro, has almost the importance of an independent movement.

† This is not intended as a depreciation of Haydn, who simply wrote in the fashion of his time ; even by Mozart, the importance of the violoncello in the *ensemble* of a piano trio was not fully recognized. Beethoven was the first to give to this instrument the position it has ever since retained.

307. Another important principle for the composer to bear in mind is, that chamber music should not be orchestral in character. In orchestral music, in which much of the effect is produced by great masses of sound, breadth and fullness are aimed at ; in chamber music, on the other hand, finish of detail and delicacy of treatment are important considerations. In this respect even eminent composers occasionally go astray. Mendelssohn has done this in parts of his octett, and especially in the first movement of his string quartett in D, Op. 44, No. 1, and in his quartett in F minor, Op. 80. Many passages in these works appear, both in conception and in treatment (*e.g.*, the frequent and long-continued employment of the *tremolo*), to be designed for the full orchestra, rather than for solo instruments. The middle parts are often mere harmonic fillings-up. A quartett—and the same remark will apply to other forms of chamber music—should be like the conversation of intimate friends, not like the noise of a great crowd.

308. After what has been said in earlier parts of this work, it may perhaps be superfluous to remind the young composer that, whether he be writing for the full orchestra or only for single instruments, he must conceive the music in the first instance for the instruments to which he is going to give it. Yet this point is so important, and so frequently disregarded by beginners, that it cannot be too strongly insisted on. If a man is writing for orchestra, he must "think orchestra"; if he is writing for a string quartett, he must "think quartett." No effective work can be produced by first inventing abstract musical themes, and afterwards deciding to what instruments they are to be allotted. In the matter of chamber music, which we are now treating, the student's imagination will be best stimulated, and guided in the right direction, first, by hearing as many trios, quartetts, &c., as possible, and next by studying all the scores of chamber music to which he can get access.* He must, in fact, adopt the same plan here which we have so frequently recommended with orchestral music.

309. We have now to speak of the principal varieties of chamber music. Taking first those kinds in which the piano takes no part, the works may be either for strings alone, for wind alone, or for strings and wind combined. Of these three subdivisions, the first is by far the most important and the most frequently employed. Many compositions exist for from two to eight stringed instruments ; but the very large majority of these are quartetts for two violins, viola, and violoncello. The reason for this is not far to seek. Four-part writing is the very founda-

---

* Nearly all the best chamber music, excepting sonatas for piano and violin, &c., is now published in score in the cheap Payne Edition ; most of the sonatas are in the Peters Edition.

tion of musical composition ; and a quartet for four strings
possesses many advantages over any other combination for the
same number of instruments.   Some of these are enumerated in
§§ 56, 57 of our first volume ; but in addition to these is one not
there referred to—the homogeneity of tone between the instruments
composing the group.   Of course, as the student already knows,
there are slight differences of quality between the violin, the viola,
and the violoncello ; but these are insignificant compared with
the differences that exist between different kinds of wind instruments, such as, for instance, the oboe and clarinet.   Moreover,
the tone of the strings does not so soon pall upon the ear as that
of the wind.

310. The fact that the element of contrast of colour, about
which so much has been said in the present volume, is almost
entirely wanting in the string quartett, deprives the composer of
one of his chief resources, and compels him to seek for variety in
other directions.   One of the most important and most serviceable
of these is the *contrapuntal* treatment of the instruments.   We are
not using the adjective in the strict technical sense in which it is
so often employed in speaking of fugues, &c., but in its wider
acceptation, as meaning the combination of independent melodies.
If we compare the second violin and viola parts of one of Haydn's
quartetts with those of one of his symphonies, we shall find that,
as a whole, there is decidedly more life and more melody in the
former than in the latter.   This, it should be added, is only a
generalization ; many passages are to be found, even in the best
quartetts, in which the middle parts of the harmony are mere
accompaniment ; and, even for the sake of contrast, this is advisable, as affording relief from the strain on the attention that
would result, were four melodies continually going on simultaneously.

311. Another means of obtaining contrast in quartett-writing
is the alternation of full and thin harmony.   Just as, in orchestral
writing, no composer of any judgment would think of keeping all
the instruments continually at work, so in a quartett three-part,
and even two-part harmony should be used from time to time, for
the sake of variety.   On the other hand, when fullness is required,
as the instruments are all *solo* instruments, double-stopping, if
judiciously written, may be more freely introduced than would be
expedient in orchestral writing.

312. Another hint to be given to the student is, the extreme
importance of finished part-writing.   In an orchestral score, it is
often possible for some slipshod and even crude work to pass
unnoticed in performance, from being concealed beneath the
fullness of the harmony, or the richness of the instrumentation.
But with only the four parts of a string quartett, every note will be
distinctly heard, and the utmost purity of part-writing becomes
imperative.

313. We have already incidentally spoken of the desirability of not writing orchestrally for chamber music ; and this applies with special force to the string quartett. It is impossible to give an exact definition of what constitutes an orchestral style of writing ; this is a matter that can be more easily felt than described. The student will best acquire the knowledge by carefully comparing the quartetts, say of Mozart or Beethoven, with the symphonies of the same composers. In no form of composition is thematic development (see *Applied Forms*, chap. viii.) of more importance than in this ; great care should therefore be taken in the selection of the subject-matter to be treated. For the various reasons we have given, we consider that it is far more difficult to write a good quartett than a good symphony.

314. Next to the quartett, the quintett is the most common combination for stringed instruments. In the large majority of string quintetts the additional instrument is a second viola, as in the quintetts of Mozart, Beethoven, Spohr, and Mendelssohn ; occasionally, instead of a second viola, a second violoncello is added. Schubert's magnificent quintett in C, Op. 163, is the finest and best known example of the latter combination. In some of Onslow's quintetts a double-bass is used instead of a second violoncello.

315. The character of the ensemble in a quintett differs somewhat from that of a quartett, owing to the greater prominence of viola or violoncello tone ; but nearly all that has been said about the quartett applies with equal force. It should, however, be mentioned that in the best examples, such as the quintetts of Mozart and Beethoven, it is comparatively rare to find real five-part harmony long continued. Rests in some of the parts are more frequent than in quartetts—and when all the instruments are employed, we still often find only four-part harmony—the first violin being doubled in the lower octave, either by the second, or by one of the violas.

316. This is still more the case if the number of instruments be still further increased, as in the sextett (two violins, two violas, and two violoncellos), or the octett (four violins, two violas, and two violoncellos). Not many works of this kind exist ; when the number of five instruments is exceeded, some wind are mostly added to the strings. In sextetts and octetts for strings only, the instruments are either used chiefly in alternation, or, when all are employed, some parts are usually doubled, either in the unison or in the octave. An examination of the score of Mendelssohn's octett, the finest example of its class, will show the student how very little real eight-part writing there is in the work. As was incidentally said (§ 307), much of the music is quite orchestral in character.

317. Spohr's four double quartetts* are rather different in their

---

* Published in score in the Payne Edition.

treatment; and, considered as chamber music, we think, more successful than the octett of which we have just spoken. In these works each quartett is complete in itself, and much of the effect is obtained by the antiphony of the two. When they are employed together, the one often has merely an accompaniment of simple harmony to the imitative counterpoint of the other. There is little or no trace here of the orchestral style, and the works are models of pure and finished part-writing.

318. If the number of stringed instruments be reduced below four, the composer is confronted by a difficulty of another kind. It is now impossible to obtain four-part harmony without 'double-stopping,' which evidently is not always available. In string trios, therefore, in which the instruments are mostly violin, viola, and violoncello, more rarely two violins and violoncello,* it is mostly necessary to make considerable use of broken chords and arpeggios in the middle of the harmony. As the best models for the student may be recommended the beautiful trio in E flat by Mozart, and Beethoven's four string trios, and Serenade Trio, Op. 8.

319. It is obvious that with duos for strings (two violins, or violin and viola) the composer's resources will be still more restricted. Yet the study of Mozart's two duos for violin and viola, and of Spohr's duos for two violins, will show that, by the exercise of due ingenuity, a far richer and fuller effect is possible, even with two instruments, than would appear at first sight.

320. Chamber music for wind instruments alone is far less common than that for strings, and requires a different kind of treatment. It is very seldom that works have been composed for wind instruments of the same kind, though Kuhlau has written a quartett for four flutes, and Kummer has published twelve trios for three bassoons. But, in most cases, instruments of different tone-quality are combined, and instead of homogeneity, as with the strings, we have contrast of colouring. The first question that presents itself is, What wind instruments should be chosen for chamber music? One would hardly think of using the rich and sonorous trombone; for it would be very difficult in a work of any extent to combine it effectively with the softer reed instruments. The trumpet also, though it has been occasionally employed (e.g., in Hummel's 'Military Septett'), could very seldom be introduced with advantage. The best instruments to use will be the reed instruments, the flutes, and the horns, as these are capable of most expression, and (except, perhaps, the horns) of most execution.

321. As wind instruments can only produce one note at a time, it is very seldom advisable to write for fewer than four or five; and in the larger number of works of this class, six or eight are found. As exceptional cases may be cited Beethoven's three

---

* Dvořák has written an interesting trio for two violins and viola; but this combination lies under the disadvantage of having no bass below tenor C.

duos for clarinet and bassoon—among the less interesting of his works—and the little Trio, Op. 87, for two oboes and cor anglais. The larger number of Mozart's Divertimenti for wind alone are written for two oboes, two bassoons, and two horns, to which he sometimes adds two clarinets (see Ex. 39 of this volume), and in two cases two corni inglesi as well.   It is worth noticing that neither Mozart nor Beethoven uses flutes in any of the chamber music written for wind instruments only.

322. The predominance of oboe tone to be found in most of Mozart's chamber music for wind instruments is probably due to the fact that in the last century the clarinet was much less frequently used than at present.   In Beethoven's only sextett for wind instruments (Op. 71), there are no oboes, the work being written for two clarinets, two bassoons, and two horns—a decidedly preferable combination to Mozart's, as the instruments blend better (see § 45), and a long continuance of oboe tone soon becomes wearisome.

323. If the student wishes to write for wind instruments alone, we should advise two clarinets, two bassoons, and two horns, as the smallest expedient combination; to this may be added, if desired, two oboes, or (better still) one oboe and one flute, which not only gives a larger compass upwards, but an additional tone-colour.   Beyond eight instruments it is hardly desirable to go ; with a larger number the music may easily become too orchestral in character.

324. If the sonata form is adopted in compositions for wind only, it should generally be concise.   Too lengthy movements are alike fatiguing to players and hearers ; for, as already mentioned, the tone of the wind palls upon the ear much sooner than that of the strings.   It is probably for this reason that in works of this kind the smaller forms, rather than the larger, are so frequently met with.

325. Only a few words are needful concerning compositions for strings and wind combined.   There may be but one wind instrument, as in the clarinet quintetts of Mozart, Weber, and Brahms ; or there may be several, as in the septett of Beethoven, the octett of Schubert, and the nonett of Spohr.   In the latter a variety of colouring is obtainable which approximates to that of the orchestra.   The same general principles which have been laid down in speaking of chamber music for strings alone apply here also, and the student will best learn how to treat such combinations by examining the scores of as many works of this kind as he is able to procure.

326. In chamber music with the piano, other considerations have to be taken into account.   The student already knows that the piano differs from nearly all other instruments in its inability to sustain sounds at a uniform strength, and that, as a compensation, it is able by itself to give full harmony.   Its quality of tone,

also, while strongly contrasted both with strings and wind, is able to blend equally well with either. When combined with one stringed instrument—violin or violoncello, more rarely the viola—the two instruments should be alternately prominent. As an illustration of what is meant, let the student examine the opening of Beethoven's sonata in F, for piano and violin. Here he will see the first subject announced by the violin, with an arpeggio accompaniment for the piano; on the completion of the sentence, the parts are reversed, the piano taking the melody, and the violin the accompaniment. Frequently also, as in the Rondo of the same work, the subject is first announced by the piano alone, and then repeated by the violin.

327. If one of the instruments have merely accompaniment, care should be taken (especially with the piano) that this does not degenerate into mere meaningless passage-work. We do not mean by this that arpeggios and similar figures are to be altogether avoided ; but it is best in many cases to give the accompaniment a quasi-contrapuntal character, especially in *allegro* movements. One of the finest models of this method of treatment will be found in Beethoven's great sonata for piano and violin in C minor, Op. 30, No. 2, which deserves careful examination.

328. In a duet for piano and violoncello, much more use should be made of the latter for melodic purposes than is customary in orchestral writing. It is also frequently very effective to give the real bass of the harmony to the violoncello, as Mendelssohn has done in the first movement of his sonata in D, Op, 58, at the seventeenth bar. At the twenty-first bar of the finale of the same work will be found a fine example of the resonant *pizzicato* of the low notes of the cello employed in the same way.

329. As all chamber music is written for *solo* instruments, larger demands may be made on the technique of the string players than would be expedient or safe with the orchestra. Thus, in the scherzo of Beethoven's sonata in A, Op. 69, for piano and violoncello, are found 'double-stops' in sixths and thirds, which are essentially solo passages. The same thing may be said of the chords for the violin with which the 'Kreutzer Sonata' opens. It will, however, be advisable to make but sparing use of such effects.

330. If more than one instrument is employed with the piano, the name 'Sonata' is not now used.* The works are described as trios, quartetts, &c., according to the number of instruments taking part in them. With every additional instrument introduced, the resources at the disposal of the composer are increased. Even in pianoforte trios, by the judicious use of 'double-stops,' it is possible to obtain alternations of full harmony for piano and strings,

---

* Formerly, when the strings had less important parts than in the present day pianoforte trios were often described as 'Sonatas for piano, with accompaniment for the violin and violoncello.'

Excellent examples of this may be seen in the third movement of Beethoven's trio, Op. 70, No. 2, and in the two trios of Schubert. With piano quartetts and quintetts this is one of the commonest, as well as most effective devices (see, especially Mozart's piano quartett in G minor, and the quintetts of Schubert, Schumann, Brahms, and Dvořák).

331. It is quite impossible to enumerate even a small part of the effects obtainable by the combination of the piano with strings. The only way to learn them is that which we have so continually to recommend in this volume—the study of the best models. Let the student make himself thoroughly acquainted with the trios of Beethoven, Schubert, Mendelssohn, and Schumann, the quartetts of Mozart, Schumann, and Brahms, and the quintetts named at the end of the last paragraph, and he will know far more about the subject than he would learn from anything that could be written in this volume.

332. It was said in § 104 that a single wind instrument was more powerful than a single violin ; this is probably one chief reason why the combination of wind instruments with the piano is so much rarer than that of strings. Excepting in the case of a sonata for piano with one wind instrument (*e.g.*, Beethoven's sonata, Op. 17, for piano and horn, Weber's ' Duo Concertante,' Op. 48, for piano and clarinet, and Brahms's two sonatas, Op. 120, for the same instruments), it is rare to find fewer than four wind instruments employed ;* probably because with a smaller number full harmony for the wind cannot be obtained. The four instruments usually employed are either the oboe, clarinet, bassoon, and horn, as in the quintetts of Mozart and Beethoven ; or the flute, clarinet, bassoon, and horn, as in those of Spohr and Rubinstein.

333. Owing to the fuller tone of wind instruments, there is always more danger of their overpowering the piano than is the case with strings. We therefore seldom, if ever, find the wind employed, as the strings so often are, to furnish a mere accompaniment, of more or less importance, to the piano. To the student who wishes to understand the different treatment of strings and wind, when combined with the piano, it will be highly interesting and instructive to compare Beethoven's quintett, Op. 16, for piano and wind, spoken of in the last paragraph, with the composer's later arrangement of the same work as a quartett for piano and strings. It will be seen that not only are the melodies frequently ornamented in the later version, but that many passages, which in the quintett are allotted to the piano alone, have a light accompaniment for the strings added to them in the quartett.

334. If the two quintetts of Mozart and Beethoven are compared, it will be found that in the former the upper part for the wind instruments is mostly given to the oboe, and in the latter to

---

* The only examples we can remember to the contrary are Glinka's trio for piano, clarinet, and bassoon ; and a trio by Reinecke for piano, oboe, and horn.

the clarinet. The probable explanation is, that Mozart in most of his concerted music for wind instruments gives the leading part to the oboe. That he knew quite well the effect of which the clarinet was capable he often showed in other works, such as the clarinet quintett; the oboe seems to have been an instrument of his special personal predilection, and the importance of the clarinet was hardly fully recognized before Beethoven. If the student wishes to write a quintett for piano and wind, it will be well for him to give both instruments an equal share in the work.

335. The combination of the piano with both stringed and wind instruments is comparatively rare. Beethoven and Brahms have written trios for piano, clarinet, and violoncello; though both are interesting, neither will rank among the greatest works of its composer. Much more successful is the trio by Mozart for the unusual combination of piano, clarinet, and viola, a work in which a number of novel effects of tone-colour will be found, and with which every musician ought to be acquainted. Schumann's four 'Märchenerzählungen' (Op. 132), for the same combination of instruments, are less successful.

336. If the piano be combined with several wind and stringed instruments, as in a septett, there is considerable risk of its being overpowered altogether, unless it be treated in the style of a concerto. Several such works exist, the best known being the formerly extremely popular septett in D minor by Hummel, for piano, flute, oboe, horn, viola, violoncello, and double-bass. In this work, one of its composer's best, though now out of fashion and seldom heard, the pianoforte part is extremely brilliant, and the parts for the other instruments are, as a whole, of subordinate importance. The work, in four movements, has the regular form of a trio or quartett, but in its style it resembles rather a concerto with accompaniment for only a few instruments than what is generally understood by concerted chamber music. It will be hardly advisable for students to experiment in similar directions.

337. It was originally intended to deal with the subject of chamber music at considerably greater length, and to give examples of characteristic passages for the various combinations of which we have spoken. This volume, however, has already extended to so much greater length than was anticipated, that it has been necessary to condense this portion of the work, and to confine ourselves to pointing out to the student where he can find examples and models on which to work. Here, therefore, our task ends. While we have endeavoured to lay down general principles for the guidance of the learner, it has been quite impossible to do more. The field is too wide to be entirely traversed in any text-book; new experiments in orchestration are continually being tried—some of them brilliant successes, others hardly less brilliant failures. There is also a steady growth in the orchestra itself, initiated by Wagner and Liszt, imitated and carried

on by some of the younger composers of the present day.   Nor can it be said that the limit is yet reached ; for there is no finality in art.   Let the student by all means, if he wishes, experiment in writing for the large modern orchestra ; but let him not forget that a great composer does not necessarily require an enormous mass of instruments to produce a great effect.   Some of the most lovely pieces of scoring to be found in the examples given in these two volumes are those in which comparatively few instruments are employed.

338.   Our final word will be one of warning.   Let the student on no account imagine that the mere study of these volumes will be sufficient to enable him to write well for the orchestra.   No book ever written can teach this unaided.   Orchestral music must be heard as often as possible, and the scores of the great masters must be carefully and closely studied.   If, in addition, the student has the opportunity of hearing some of his own attempts at scoring played on the orchestra—an opportunity, unfortunately, mostly restricted to the students of our large music schools—the experience he will gain will be invaluable.   But even without this, much can be done by conscientious work ; and if the young musician have a natural feeling for tone-colour, he may learn, by imitating good models, to score effectively, even if not brilliantly.

THE END.

ANALYTICAL INDEX.

✱ *The numbers refer to the* paragraphs, *not the pages.*

—◦◆◦—

MUSICAL ILLUSTRATIONS.

A CATALOG OF SELECTED
DOVER BOOKS
IN ALL FIELDS OF INTEREST

A CATALOG OF SELECTED DOVER
BOOKS IN ALL FIELDS OF INTEREST

CONCERNING THE SPIRITUAL IN ART, Wassily Kandinsky. Pioneering work by father of abstract art. Thoughts on color theory, nature of art. Analysis of earlier masters. 12 illustrations. 80pp. of text. 5⅜ x 8½.   23411-8

ANIMALS: 1,419 Copyright-Free Illustrations of Mammals, Birds, Fish, Insects, etc., Jim Harter (ed.). Clear wood engravings present, in extremely lifelike poses, over 1,000 species of animals. One of the most extensive pictorial sourcebooks of its kind. Captions. Index. 284pp. 9 x 12.   23766-4

CELTIC ART: The Methods of Construction, George Bain. Simple geometric techniques for making Celtic interlacements, spirals, Kells-type initials, animals, humans, etc. Over 500 illustrations. 160pp. 9 x 12. (Available in U.S. only.)   22923-8

AN ATLAS OF ANATOMY FOR ARTISTS, Fritz Schider. Most thorough reference work on art anatomy in the world. Hundreds of illustrations, including selections from works by Vesalius, Leonardo, Goya, Ingres, Michelangelo, others. 593 illustrations. 192pp. 7⅛ x 10¼.   20241-0

CELTIC HAND STROKE-BY-STROKE (Irish Half-Uncial from "The Book of Kells"): An Arthur Baker Calligraphy Manual, Arthur Baker. Complete guide to creating each letter of the alphabet in distinctive Celtic manner. Covers hand position, strokes, pens, inks, paper, more. Illustrated. 48pp. 8¼ x 11.   24336-2

EASY ORIGAMI, John Montroll. Charming collection of 32 projects (hat, cup, pelican, piano, swan, many more) specially designed for the novice origami hobbyist. Clearly illustrated easy-to-follow instructions insure that even beginning papercrafters will achieve successful results. 48pp. 8¼ x 11.   27298-2

THE COMPLETE BOOK OF BIRDHOUSE CONSTRUCTION FOR WOODWORKERS, Scott D. Campbell. Detailed instructions, illustrations, tables. Also data on bird habitat and instinct patterns. Bibliography. 3 tables. 63 illustrations in 15 figures. 48pp. 5¼ x 8½.   24407-5

BLOOMINGDALE'S ILLUSTRATED 1886 CATALOG: Fashions, Dry Goods and Housewares, Bloomingdale Brothers. Famed merchants' extremely rare catalog depicting about 1,700 products: clothing, housewares, firearms, dry goods, jewelry, more. Invaluable for dating, identifying vintage items. Also, copyright-free graphics for artists, designers. Co-published with Henry Ford Museum & Greenfield Village. 160pp. 8¼ x 11.   25780-0

HISTORIC COSTUME IN PICTURES, Braun & Schneider. Over 1,450 costumed figures in clearly detailed engravings–from dawn of civilization to end of 19th century. Captions. Many folk costumes. 256pp. 8⅜ x 11¾.   23150-X

STICKLEY CRAFTSMAN FURNITURE CATALOGS, Gustav Stickley and L. & J. G. Stickley. Beautiful, functional furniture in two authentic catalogs from 1910. 594 illustrations, including 277 photos, show settles, rockers, armchairs, reclining chairs, bookcases, desks, tables. 183pp. 6½ x 9¼. 23838-5

AMERICAN LOCOMOTIVES IN HISTORIC PHOTOGRAPHS: 1858 to 1949, Ron Ziel (ed.). A rare collection of 126 meticulously detailed official photographs, called "builder portraits," of American locomotives that majestically chronicle the rise of steam locomotive power in America. Introduction. Detailed captions. xi+ 129pp. 9 x 12. 27393-8

AMERICA'S LIGHTHOUSES: An Illustrated History, Francis Ross Holland, Jr. Delightfully written, profusely illustrated fact-filled survey of over 200 American lighthouses since 1716. History, anecdotes, technological advances, more. 240pp. 8 x 10¾. 25576-X

TOWARDS A NEW ARCHITECTURE, Le Corbusier. Pioneering manifesto by founder of "International School." Technical and aesthetic theories, views of industry, economics, relation of form to function, "mass-production split" and much more. Profusely illustrated. 320pp. 6⅛ x 9¼. (Available in U.S. only.) 25023-7

HOW THE OTHER HALF LIVES, Jacob Riis. Famous journalistic record, exposing poverty and degradation of New York slums around 1900, by major social reformer. 100 striking and influential photographs. 233pp. 10 x 7⅞. 22012-5

FRUIT KEY AND TWIG KEY TO TREES AND SHRUBS, William M. Harlow. One of the handiest and most widely used identification aids. Fruit key covers 120 deciduous and evergreen species; twig key 160 deciduous species. Easily used. Over 300 photographs. 126pp. 5⅜ x 8½. 20511-8

COMMON BIRD SONGS, Dr. Donald J. Borror. Songs of 60 most common U.S. birds: robins, sparrows, cardinals, bluejays, finches, more–arranged in order of increasing complexity. Up to 9 variations of songs of each species. Cassette and manual 99911-4

ORCHIDS AS HOUSE PLANTS, Rebecca Tyson Northen. Grow cattleyas and many other kinds of orchids–in a window, in a case, or under artificial light. 63 illustrations. 148pp. 5⅜ x 8½. 23261-1

MONSTER MAZES, Dave Phillips. Masterful mazes at four levels of difficulty. Avoid deadly perils and evil creatures to find magical treasures. Solutions for all 32 exciting illustrated puzzles. 48pp. 8¼ x 11. 26005-4

MOZART'S DON GIOVANNI (DOVER OPERA LIBRETTO SERIES), Wolfgang Amadeus Mozart. Introduced and translated by Ellen H. Bleiler. Standard Italian libretto, with complete English translation. Convenient and thoroughly portable–an ideal companion for reading along with a recording or the performance itself. Introduction. List of characters. Plot summary. 121pp. 5¼ x 8½. 24944-1

TECHNICAL MANUAL AND DICTIONARY OF CLASSICAL BALLET, Gail Grant. Defines, explains, comments on steps, movements, poses and concepts. 15-page pictorial section. Basic book for student, viewer. 127pp. 5⅜ x 8½. 21843-0

THE CLARINET AND CLARINET PLAYING, David Pino. Lively, comprehensive work features suggestions about technique, musicianship, and musical interpretation, as well as guidelines for teaching, making your own reeds, and preparing for public performance. Includes an intriguing look at clarinet history. "A godsend," *The Clarinet*, Journal of the International Clarinet Society. Appendixes. 7 illus. 320pp. 5⅜ x 8½. 40270-3

HOLLYWOOD GLAMOR PORTRAITS, John Kobal (ed.). 145 photos from 1926-49. Harlow, Gable, Bogart, Bacall; 94 stars in all. Full background on photographers, technical aspects. 160pp. 8⅜ x 11¼. 23352-9

THE ANNOTATED CASEY AT THE BAT: A Collection of Ballads about the Mighty Casey/Third, Revised Edition, Martin Gardner (ed.). Amusing sequels and parodies of one of America's best-loved poems: Casey's Revenge, Why Casey Whiffed, Casey's Sister at the Bat, others. 256pp. 5⅜ x 8½. 28598-7

THE RAVEN AND OTHER FAVORITE POEMS, Edgar Allan Poe. Over 40 of the author's most memorable poems: "The Bells," "Ulalume," "Israfel," "To Helen," "The Conqueror Worm," "Eldorado," "Annabel Lee," many more. Alphabetic lists of titles and first lines. 64pp. 5³⁄₁₆ x 8¼. 26685-0

PERSONAL MEMOIRS OF U. S. GRANT, Ulysses Simpson Grant. Intelligent, deeply moving firsthand account of Civil War campaigns, considered by many the finest military memoirs ever written. Includes letters, historic photographs, maps and more. 528pp. 6⅛ x 9¼. 28587-1

ANCIENT EGYPTIAN MATERIALS AND INDUSTRIES, A. Lucas and J. Harris. Fascinating, comprehensive, thoroughly documented text describes this ancient civilization's vast resources and the processes that incorporated them in daily life, including the use of animal products, building materials, cosmetics, perfumes and incense, fibers, glazed ware, glass and its manufacture, materials used in the mummification process, and much more. 544pp. 6⅛ x 9¼. (Available in U.S. only.) 40446-3

RUSSIAN STORIES/RUSSKIE RASSKAZY: A Dual-Language Book, edited by Gleb Struve. Twelve tales by such masters as Chekhov, Tolstoy, Dostoevsky, Pushkin, others. Excellent word-for-word English translations on facing pages, plus teaching and study aids, Russian/English vocabulary, biographical/critical introductions, more. 416pp. 5⅜ x 8½. 26244-8

PHILADELPHIA THEN AND NOW: 60 Sites Photographed in the Past and Present, Kenneth Finkel and Susan Oyama. Rare photographs of City Hall, Logan Square, Independence Hall, Betsy Ross House, other landmarks juxtaposed with contemporary views. Captures changing face of historic city. Introduction. Captions. 128pp. 8¼ x 11. 25790-8

AIA ARCHITECTURAL GUIDE TO NASSAU AND SUFFOLK COUNTIES, LONG ISLAND, The American Institute of Architects, Long Island Chapter, and the Society for the Preservation of Long Island Antiquities. Comprehensive, well-researched and generously illustrated volume brings to life over three centuries of Long Island's great architectural heritage. More than 240 photographs with authoritative, extensively detailed captions. 176pp. 8¼ x 11. 26946-9

NORTH AMERICAN INDIAN LIFE: Customs and Traditions of 23 Tribes, Elsie Clews Parsons (ed.). 27 fictionalized essays by noted anthropologists examine religion, customs, government, additional facets of life among the Winnebago, Crow, Zuni, Eskimo, other tribes. 480pp. 6⅛ x 9¼. 27377-6

FRANK LLOYD WRIGHT'S DANA HOUSE, Donald Hoffmann. Pictorial essay of residential masterpiece with over 160 interior and exterior photos, plans, elevations, sketches and studies. 128pp. 9¼ x 10¾. 29120-0

THE MALE AND FEMALE FIGURE IN MOTION: 60 Classic Photographic Sequences, Eadweard Muybridge. 60 true-action photographs of men and women walking, running, climbing, bending, turning, etc., reproduced from rare 19th-century masterpiece. vi + 121pp. 9 x 12. 24745-7

1001 QUESTIONS ANSWERED ABOUT THE SEASHORE, N. J. Berrill and Jacquelyn Berrill. Queries answered about dolphins, sea snails, sponges, starfish, fishes, shore birds, many others. Covers appearance, breeding, growth, feeding, much more. 305pp. 5¼ x 8¼. 23366-9

ATTRACTING BIRDS TO YOUR YARD, William J. Weber. Easy-to-follow guide offers advice on how to attract the greatest diversity of birds: birdhouses, feeders, water and waterers, much more. 96pp. 5³⁄₁₆ x 8¼. 28927-3

MEDICINAL AND OTHER USES OF NORTH AMERICAN PLANTS: A Historical Survey with Special Reference to the Eastern Indian Tribes, Charlotte Erichsen-Brown. Chronological historical citations document 500 years of usage of plants, trees, shrubs native to eastern Canada, northeastern U.S. Also complete identifying information. 343 illustrations. 544pp. 6½ x 9¼. 25951-X

STORYBOOK MAZES, Dave Phillips. 23 stories and mazes on two-page spreads: Wizard of Oz, Treasure Island, Robin Hood, etc. Solutions. 64pp. 8¼ x 11. 23628-5

AMERICAN NEGRO SONGS: 230 Folk Songs and Spirituals, Religious and Secular, John W. Work. This authoritative study traces the African influences of songs sung and played by black Americans at work, in church, and as entertainment. The author discusses the lyric significance of such songs as "Swing Low, Sweet Chariot," "John Henry," and others and offers the words and music for 230 songs. Bibliography. Index of Song Titles. 272pp. 6½ x 9¼. 40271-1

MOVIE-STAR PORTRAITS OF THE FORTIES, John Kobal (ed.). 163 glamor, studio photos of 106 stars of the 1940s: Rita Hayworth, Ava Gardner, Marlon Brando, Clark Gable, many more. 176pp. 8⅜ x 11¼. 23546-7

BENCHLEY LOST AND FOUND, Robert Benchley. Finest humor from early 30s, about pet peeves, child psychologists, post office and others. Mostly unavailable elsewhere. 73 illustrations by Peter Arno and others. 183pp. 5⅜ x 8½. 22410-4

YEKL and THE IMPORTED BRIDEGROOM AND OTHER STORIES OF YIDDISH NEW YORK, Abraham Cahan. Film Hester Street based on *Yekl* (1896). Novel, other stories among first about Jewish immigrants on N.Y.'s East Side. 240pp. 5⅜ x 8½. 22427-9

SELECTED POEMS, Walt Whitman. Generous sampling from *Leaves of Grass*. Twenty-four poems include "I Hear America Singing," "Song of the Open Road," "I Sing the Body Electric," "When Lilacs Last in the Dooryard Bloom'd," "O Captain! My Captain!"–all reprinted from an authoritative edition. Lists of titles and first lines. 128pp. 5³⁄₁₆ x 8¼. 26878-0

THE BEST TALES OF HOFFMANN, E. T. A. Hoffmann. 10 of Hoffmann's most important stories: "Nutcracker and the King of Mice," "The Golden Flowerpot," etc. 458pp. 5⅜ x 8½.   21793-0

FROM FETISH TO GOD IN ANCIENT EGYPT, E. A. Wallis Budge. Rich detailed survey of Egyptian conception of "God" and gods, magic, cult of animals, Osiris, more. Also, superb English translations of hymns and legends. 240 illustrations. 545pp. 5⅜ x 8½.   25803-3

FRENCH STORIES/CONTES FRANÇAIS: A Dual-Language Book, Wallace Fowlie. Ten stories by French masters, Voltaire to Camus: "Micromegas" by Voltaire; "The Atheist's Mass" by Balzac; "Minuet" by de Maupassant; "The Guest" by Camus, six more. Excellent English translations on facing pages. Also French-English vocabulary list, exercises, more. 352pp. 5⅜ x 8½.   26443-2

CHICAGO AT THE TURN OF THE CENTURY IN PHOTOGRAPHS: 122 Historic Views from the Collections of the Chicago Historical Society, Larry A. Viskochil. Rare large-format prints offer detailed views of City Hall, State Street, the Loop, Hull House, Union Station, many other landmarks, circa 1904-1913. Introduction. Captions. Maps. 144pp. 9⅜ x 12¼.   24656-6

OLD BROOKLYN IN EARLY PHOTOGRAPHS, 1865-1929, William Lee Younger. Luna Park, Gravesend race track, construction of Grand Army Plaza, moving of Hotel Brighton, etc. 157 previously unpublished photographs. 165pp. 8⅞ x 11¾.
23587-4

THE MYTHS OF THE NORTH AMERICAN INDIANS, Lewis Spence. Rich anthology of the myths and legends of the Algonquins, Iroquois, Pawnees and Sioux, prefaced by an extensive historical and ethnological commentary. 36 illustrations. 480pp. 5⅜ x 8½.   25967-6

AN ENCYCLOPEDIA OF BATTLES: Accounts of Over 1,560 Battles from 1479 B.C. to the Present, David Eggenberger. Essential details of every major battle in recorded history from the first battle of Megiddo in 1479 B.C. to Grenada in 1984. List of Battle Maps. New Appendix covering the years 1967-1984. Index. 99 illustrations. 544pp. 6½ x 9¼.   24913-1

SAILING ALONE AROUND THE WORLD, Captain Joshua Slocum. First man to sail around the world, alone, in small boat. One of great feats of seamanship told in delightful manner. 67 illustrations. 294pp. 5⅜ x 8½.   20326-3

ANARCHISM AND OTHER ESSAYS, Emma Goldman. Powerful, penetrating, prophetic essays on direct action, role of minorities, prison reform, puritan hypocrisy, violence, etc. 271pp. 5⅜ x 8½.   22484-8

MYTHS OF THE HINDUS AND BUDDHISTS, Ananda K. Coomaraswamy and Sister Nivedita. Great stories of the epics; deeds of Krishna, Shiva, taken from puranas, Vedas, folk tales; etc. 32 illustrations. 400pp. 5⅜ x 8½.   21759-0

THE TRAUMA OF BIRTH, Otto Rank. Rank's controversial thesis that anxiety neurosis is caused by profound psychological trauma which occurs at birth. 256pp. 5⅜ x 8½.   27974-X

A THEOLOGICO-POLITICAL TREATISE, Benedict Spinoza. Also contains unfinished Political Treatise. Great classic on religious liberty, theory of government on common consent. R. Elwes translation. Total of 421pp. 5⅜ x 8½.   20249-6

MY BONDAGE AND MY FREEDOM, Frederick Douglass. Born a slave, Douglass became outspoken force in antislavery movement. The best of Douglass' autobiographies. Graphic description of slave life. 464pp. 5⅜ x 8½. 22457-0

FOLLOWING THE EQUATOR: A Journey Around the World, Mark Twain. Fascinating humorous account of 1897 voyage to Hawaii, Australia, India, New Zealand, etc. Ironic, bemused reports on peoples, customs, climate, flora and fauna, politics, much more. 197 illustrations. 720pp. 5⅜ x 8½. 26113-1

THE PEOPLE CALLED SHAKERS, Edward D. Andrews. Definitive study of Shakers: origins, beliefs, practices, dances, social organization, furniture and crafts, etc. 33 illustrations. 351pp. 5⅜ x 8½. 21081-2

THE MYTHS OF GREECE AND ROME, H. A. Guerber. A classic of mythology, generously illustrated, long prized for its simple, graphic, accurate retelling of the principal myths of Greece and Rome, and for its commentary on their origins and significance. With 64 illustrations by Michelangelo, Raphael, Titian, Rubens, Canova, Bernini and others. 480pp. 5⅜ x 8½. 27584-1

PSYCHOLOGY OF MUSIC, Carl E. Seashore. Classic work discusses music as a medium from psychological viewpoint. Clear treatment of physical acoustics, auditory apparatus, sound perception, development of musical skills, nature of musical feeling, host of other topics. 88 figures. 408pp. 5⅜ x 8½. 21851-1

THE PHILOSOPHY OF HISTORY, Georg W. Hegel. Great classic of Western thought develops concept that history is not chance but rational process, the evolution of freedom. 457pp. 5⅜ x 8½. 20112-0

THE BOOK OF TEA, Kakuzo Okakura. Minor classic of the Orient: entertaining, charming explanation, interpretation of traditional Japanese culture in terms of tea ceremony. 94pp. 5⅜ x 8½. 20070-1

LIFE IN ANCIENT EGYPT, Adolf Erman. Fullest, most thorough, detailed older account with much not in more recent books, domestic life, religion, magic, medicine, commerce, much more. Many illustrations reproduce tomb paintings, carvings, hieroglyphs, etc. 597pp. 5⅜ x 8½. 22632-8

SUNDIALS, Their Theory and Construction, Albert Waugh. Far and away the best, most thorough coverage of ideas, mathematics concerned, types, construction, adjusting anywhere. Simple, nontechnical treatment allows even children to build several of these dials. Over 100 illustrations. 230pp. 5⅜ x 8½. 22947-5

THEORETICAL HYDRODYNAMICS, L. M. Milne-Thomson. Classic exposition of the mathematical theory of fluid motion, applicable to both hydrodynamics and aerodynamics. Over 600 exercises. 768pp. 6⅛ x 9¼. 68970-0

SONGS OF EXPERIENCE: Facsimile Reproduction with 26 Plates in Full Color, William Blake. 26 full-color plates from a rare 1826 edition. Includes "The Tyger," "London," "Holy Thursday," and other poems. Printed text of poems. 48pp. 5¼ x 7. 24636-1

OLD-TIME VIGNETTES IN FULL COLOR, Carol Belanger Grafton (ed.). Over 390 charming, often sentimental illustrations, selected from archives of Victorian graphics—pretty women posing, children playing, food, flowers, kittens and puppies, smiling cherubs, birds and butterflies, much more. All copyright-free. 48pp. 9¼ x 12¼. 27269-9

PERSPECTIVE FOR ARTISTS, Rex Vicat Cole. Depth, perspective of sky and sea, shadows, much more, not usually covered. 391 diagrams, 81 reproductions of drawings and paintings. 279pp. 5⅜ x 8½. 22487-2

DRAWING THE LIVING FIGURE, Joseph Sheppard. Innovative approach to artistic anatomy focuses on specifics of surface anatomy, rather than muscles and bones. Over 170 drawings of live models in front, back and side views, and in widely varying poses. Accompanying diagrams. 177 illustrations. Introduction. Index. 144pp. 8⅜ x11¼. 26723-7

GOTHIC AND OLD ENGLISH ALPHABETS: 100 Complete Fonts, Dan X. Solo. Add power, elegance to posters, signs, other graphics with 100 stunning copyright-free alphabets: Blackstone, Dolbey, Germania, 97 more–including many lower-case, numerals, punctuation marks. 104pp. 8⅛ x 11. 24695-7

HOW TO DO BEADWORK, Mary White. Fundamental book on craft from simple projects to five-bead chains and woven works. 106 illustrations. 142pp. 5⅜ x 8.
20697-1

THE BOOK OF WOOD CARVING, Charles Marshall Sayers. Finest book for beginners discusses fundamentals and offers 34 designs. "Absolutely first rate . . . well thought out and well executed."–E. J. Tangerman. 118pp. 7¾ x 10⅝. 23654-4

ILLUSTRATED CATALOG OF CIVIL WAR MILITARY GOODS: Union Army Weapons, Insignia, Uniform Accessories, and Other Equipment, Schuyler, Hartley, and Graham. Rare, profusely illustrated 1846 catalog includes Union Army uniform and dress regulations, arms and ammunition, coats, insignia, flags, swords, rifles, etc. 226 illustrations. 160pp. 9 x 12. 24939-5

WOMEN'S FASHIONS OF THE EARLY 1900s: An Unabridged Republication of "New York Fashions, 1909," National Cloak & Suit Co. Rare catalog of mail-order fashions documents women's and children's clothing styles shortly after the turn of the century. Captions offer full descriptions, prices. Invaluable resource for fashion, costume historians. Approximately 725 illustrations. 128pp. 8⅜ x 11¼. 27276-1

THE 1912 AND 1915 GUSTAV STICKLEY FURNITURE CATALOGS, Gustav Stickley. With over 200 detailed illustrations and descriptions, these two catalogs are essential reading and reference materials and identification guides for Stickley furniture. Captions cite materials, dimensions and prices. 112pp. 6½ x 9¼. 26676-1

EARLY AMERICAN LOCOMOTIVES, John H. White, Jr. Finest locomotive engravings from early 19th century: historical (1804–74), main-line (after 1870), special, foreign, etc. 147 plates. 142pp. 11⅜ x 8¼. 22772-3

THE TALL SHIPS OF TODAY IN PHOTOGRAPHS, Frank O. Braynard. Lavishly illustrated tribute to nearly 100 majestic contemporary sailing vessels: Amerigo Vespucci, Clearwater, Constitution, Eagle, Mayflower, Sea Cloud, Victory, many more. Authoritative captions provide statistics, background on each ship. 190 black-and-white photographs and illustrations. Introduction. 128pp. 8⅞ x 11¾.
27163-3

LITTLE BOOK OF EARLY AMERICAN CRAFTS AND TRADES, Peter Stockham (ed.). 1807 children's book explains crafts and trades: baker, hatter, cooper, potter, and many others. 23 copperplate illustrations. 140pp. 4⅝ x 6.   23336-7

VICTORIAN FASHIONS AND COSTUMES FROM HARPER'S BAZAR, 1867–1898, Stella Blum (ed.). Day costumes, evening wear, sports clothes, shoes, hats, other accessories in over 1,000 detailed engravings. 320pp. 9⅜ x 12¼. 22990-4

GUSTAV STICKLEY, THE CRAFTSMAN, Mary Ann Smith. Superb study surveys broad scope of Stickley's achievement, especially in architecture. Design philosophy, rise and fall of the Craftsman empire, descriptions and floor plans for many Craftsman houses, more. 86 black-and-white halftones. 31 line illustrations. Introduction 208pp. 6½ x 9¼.   27210-9

THE LONG ISLAND RAIL ROAD IN EARLY PHOTOGRAPHS, Ron Ziel. Over 220 rare photos, informative text document origin (1844) and development of rail service on Long Island. Vintage views of early trains, locomotives, stations, passengers, crews, much more. Captions. 8⅞ x 11¾.   26301-0

VOYAGE OF THE LIBERDADE, Joshua Slocum. Great 19th-century mariner's thrilling, first-hand account of the wreck of his ship off South America, the 35-foot boat he built from the wreckage, and its remarkable voyage home. 128pp. 5⅜ x 8½. 40022-0

TEN BOOKS ON ARCHITECTURE, Vitruvius. The most important book ever written on architecture. Early Roman aesthetics, technology, classical orders, site selection, all other aspects. Morgan translation. 331pp. 5⅜ x 8½.   20645-9

THE HUMAN FIGURE IN MOTION, Eadweard Muybridge. More than 4,500 stopped-action photos, in action series, showing undraped men, women, children jumping, lying down, throwing, sitting, wrestling, carrying, etc. 390pp. 7⅞ x 10⅝. 20204-6 Clothbd.

TREES OF THE EASTERN AND CENTRAL UNITED STATES AND CANADA, William M. Harlow. Best one-volume guide to 140 trees. Full descriptions, woodlore, range, etc. Over 600 illustrations. Handy size. 288pp. 4½ x 6⅜.   20395-6

SONGS OF WESTERN BIRDS, Dr. Donald J. Borror. Complete song and call repertoire of 60 western species, including flycatchers, juncoes, cactus wrens, many more–includes fully illustrated booklet.   Cassette and manual 99913-0

GROWING AND USING HERBS AND SPICES, Milo Miloradovich. Versatile handbook provides all the information needed for cultivation and use of all the herbs and spices available in North America. 4 illustrations. Index. Glossary. 236pp. 5⅜ x 8½. 25058-X

BIG BOOK OF MAZES AND LABYRINTHS, Walter Shepherd. 50 mazes and labyrinths in all–classical, solid, ripple, and more–in one great volume. Perfect inexpensive puzzler for clever youngsters. Full solutions. 112pp. 8⅛ x 11.   22951-3

PIANO TUNING, J. Cree Fischer. Clearest, best book for beginner, amateur. Simple repairs, raising dropped notes, tuning by easy method of flattened fifths. No previous skills needed. 4 illustrations. 201pp. 5⅜ x 8½. 23267-0

HINTS TO SINGERS, Lillian Nordica. Selecting the right teacher, developing confidence, overcoming stage fright, and many other important skills receive thoughtful discussion in this indispensible guide, written by a world-famous diva of four decades' experience. 96pp. 5⅜ x 8½. 40094-8

THE COMPLETE NONSENSE OF EDWARD LEAR, Edward Lear. All nonsense limericks, zany alphabets, Owl and Pussycat, songs, nonsense botany, etc., illustrated by Lear. Total of 320pp. 5⅜ x 8½. (Available in U.S. only.) 20167-8

VICTORIAN PARLOUR POETRY: An Annotated Anthology, Michael R. Turner. 117 gems by Longfellow, Tennyson, Browning, many lesser-known poets. "The Village Blacksmith," "Curfew Must Not Ring Tonight," "Only a Baby Small," dozens more, often difficult to find elsewhere. Index of poets, titles, first lines. xxiii + 325pp. 5⅝ x 8¼. 27044-0

DUBLINERS, James Joyce. Fifteen stories offer vivid, tightly focused observations of the lives of Dublin's poorer classes. At least one, "The Dead," is considered a masterpiece. Reprinted complete and unabridged from standard edition. 160pp. $5\frac{3}{16}$ x 8¼. 26870-5

GREAT WEIRD TALES: 14 Stories by Lovecraft, Blackwood, Machen and Others, S. T. Joshi (ed.). 14 spellbinding tales, including "The Sin Eater," by Fiona McLeod, "The Eye Above the Mantel," by Frank Belknap Long, as well as renowned works by R. H. Barlow, Lord Dunsany, Arthur Machen, W. C. Morrow and eight other masters of the genre. 256pp. 5⅜ x 8½. (Available in U.S. only.) 40436-6

THE BOOK OF THE SACRED MAGIC OF ABRAMELIN THE MAGE, translated by S. MacGregor Mathers. Medieval manuscript of ceremonial magic. Basic document in Aleister Crowley, Golden Dawn groups. 268pp. 5⅜ x 8½. 23211-5

NEW RUSSIAN-ENGLISH AND ENGLISH-RUSSIAN DICTIONARY, M. A. O'Brien. This is a remarkably handy Russian dictionary, containing a surprising amount of information, including over 70,000 entries. 366pp. 4½ x 6⅛. 20208-9

HISTORIC HOMES OF THE AMERICAN PRESIDENTS, Second, Revised Edition, Irvin Haas. A traveler's guide to American Presidential homes, most open to the public, depicting and describing homes occupied by every American President from George Washington to George Bush. With visiting hours, admission charges, travel routes. 175 photographs. Index. 160pp. 8¼ x 11. 26751-2

NEW YORK IN THE FORTIES, Andreas Feininger. 162 brilliant photographs by the well-known photographer, formerly with *Life* magazine. Commuters, shoppers, Times Square at night, much else from city at its peak. Captions by John von Hartz. 181pp. 9¼ x 10¾. 23585-8

INDIAN SIGN LANGUAGE, William Tomkins. Over 525 signs developed by Sioux and other tribes. Written instructions and diagrams. Also 290 pictographs. 111pp. 6⅛ x 9¼. 22029-X

ANATOMY: A Complete Guide for Artists, Joseph Sheppard. A master of figure drawing shows artists how to render human anatomy convincingly. Over 460 illustrations. 224pp. 8⅜ x 11¼.
27279-6

MEDIEVAL CALLIGRAPHY: Its History and Technique, Marc Drogin. Spirited history, comprehensive instruction manual covers 13 styles (ca. 4th century through 15th). Excellent photographs; directions for duplicating medieval techniques with modern tools. 224pp. 8⅜ x 11¼.
26142-5

DRIED FLOWERS: How to Prepare Them, Sarah Whitlock and Martha Rankin. Complete instructions on how to use silica gel, meal and borax, perlite aggregate, sand and borax, glycerine and water to create attractive permanent flower arrangements. 12 illustrations. 32pp. 5⅜ x 8½.
21802-3

EASY-TO-MAKE BIRD FEEDERS FOR WOODWORKERS, Scott D. Campbell. Detailed, simple-to-use guide for designing, constructing, caring for and using feeders. Text, illustrations for 12 classic and contemporary designs. 96pp. 5⅜ x 8½.
25847-5

SCOTTISH WONDER TALES FROM MYTH AND LEGEND, Donald A. Mackenzie. 16 lively tales tell of giants rumbling down mountainsides, of a magic wand that turns stone pillars into warriors, of gods and goddesses, evil hags, powerful forces and more. 240pp. 5⅜ x 8½.
29677-6

THE HISTORY OF UNDERCLOTHES, C. Willett Cunnington and Phyllis Cunnington. Fascinating, well-documented survey covering six centuries of English undergarments, enhanced with over 100 illustrations: 12th-century laced-up bodice, footed long drawers (1795), 19th-century bustles, 19th-century corsets for men, Victorian "bust improvers," much more. 272pp. 5⅜ x 8¼.
27124-2

ARTS AND CRAFTS FURNITURE: The Complete Brooks Catalog of 1912, Brooks Manufacturing Co. Photos and detailed descriptions of more than 150 now very collectible furniture designs from the Arts and Crafts movement depict davenports, settees, buffets, desks, tables, chairs, bedsteads, dressers and more, all built of solid, quarter-sawed oak. Invaluable for students and enthusiasts of antiques, Americana and the decorative arts. 80pp. 6½ x 9¼.
27471-3

WILBUR AND ORVILLE: A Biography of the Wright Brothers, Fred Howard. Definitive, crisply written study tells the full story of the brothers' lives and work. A vividly written biography, unparalleled in scope and color, that also captures the spirit of an extraordinary era. 560pp. 6⅛ x 9¼.
40297-5

THE ARTS OF THE SAILOR: Knotting, Splicing and Ropework, Hervey Garrett Smith. Indispensable shipboard reference covers tools, basic knots and useful hitches; handsewing and canvas work, more. Over 100 illustrations. Delightful reading for sea lovers. 256pp. 5⅜ x 8½.
26440-8

FRANK LLOYD WRIGHT'S FALLINGWATER: The House and Its History, Second, Revised Edition, Donald Hoffmann. A total revision–both in text and illustrations–of the standard document on Fallingwater, the boldest, most personal architectural statement of Wright's mature years, updated with valuable new material from the recently opened Frank Lloyd Wright Archives. "Fascinating"–*The New York Times.* 116 illustrations. 128pp. 9¼ x 10¾.
27430-6

PHOTOGRAPHIC SKETCHBOOK OF THE CIVIL WAR, Alexander Gardner. 100 photos taken on field during the Civil War. Famous shots of Manassas Harper's Ferry, Lincoln, Richmond, slave pens, etc. 244pp. 10⅝ x 8¼. 22731-6

FIVE ACRES AND INDEPENDENCE, Maurice G. Kains. Great back-to-the-land classic explains basics of self-sufficient farming. The one book to get. 95 illustrations. 397pp. 5⅜ x 8½. 20974-1

SONGS OF EASTERN BIRDS, Dr. Donald J. Borror. Songs and calls of 60 species most common to eastern U.S.: warblers, woodpeckers, flycatchers, thrushes, larks, many more in high-quality recording. Cassette and manual 99912-2

A MODERN HERBAL, Margaret Grieve. Much the fullest, most exact, most useful compilation of herbal material. Gigantic alphabetical encyclopedia, from aconite to zedoary, gives botanical information, medical properties, folklore, economic uses, much else. Indispensable to serious reader. 161 illustrations. 888pp. 6½ x 9¼. 2-vol. set. (Available in U.S. only.) Vol. I: 22798-7
Vol. II: 22799-5

HIDDEN TREASURE MAZE BOOK, Dave Phillips. Solve 34 challenging mazes accompanied by heroic tales of adventure. Evil dragons, people-eating plants, blood-thirsty giants, many more dangerous adversaries lurk at every twist and turn. 34 mazes, stories, solutions. 48pp. 8¼ x 11. 24566-7

LETTERS OF W. A. MOZART, Wolfgang A. Mozart. Remarkable letters show bawdy wit, humor, imagination, musical insights, contemporary musical world; includes some letters from Leopold Mozart. 276pp. 5⅜ x 8½. 22859-2

BASIC PRINCIPLES OF CLASSICAL BALLET, Agrippina Vaganova. Great Russian theoretician, teacher explains methods for teaching classical ballet. 118 illustrations. 175pp. 5⅜ x 8½. 22036-2

THE JUMPING FROG, Mark Twain. Revenge edition. The original story of The Celebrated Jumping Frog of Calaveras County, a hapless French translation, and Twain's hilarious "retranslation" from the French. 12 illustrations. 66pp. 5⅜ x 8½. 22686-7

BEST REMEMBERED POEMS, Martin Gardner (ed.). The 126 poems in this superb collection of 19th- and 20th-century British and American verse range from Shelley's "To a Skylark" to the impassioned "Renascence" of Edna St. Vincent Millay and to Edward Lear's whimsical "The Owl and the Pussycat." 224pp. 5⅜ x 8½. 27165-X

COMPLETE SONNETS, William Shakespeare. Over 150 exquisite poems deal with love, friendship, the tyranny of time, beauty's evanescence, death and other themes in language of remarkable power, precision and beauty. Glossary of archaic terms. 80pp. 5$\frac{3}{16}$ x 8¼. 26686-9

THE BATTLES THAT CHANGED HISTORY, Fletcher Pratt. Eminent historian profiles 16 crucial conflicts, ancient to modern, that changed the course of civilization. 352pp. 5⅜ x 8½. 41129-X

THE WIT AND HUMOR OF OSCAR WILDE, Alvin Redman (ed.). More than 1,000 ripostes, paradoxes, wisecracks: Work is the curse of the drinking classes; I can resist everything except temptation; etc. 258pp. 5⅜ x 8½.   20602-5

SHAKESPEARE LEXICON AND QUOTATION DICTIONARY, Alexander Schmidt. Full definitions, locations, shades of meaning in every word in plays and poems. More than 50,000 exact quotations. 1,485pp. 6½ x 9¼. 2-vol. set.
Vol. 1: 22726-X
Vol. 2: 22727-8

SELECTED POEMS, Emily Dickinson. Over 100 best-known, best-loved poems by one of America's foremost poets, reprinted from authoritative early editions. No comparable edition at this price. Index of first lines. 64pp. 5³⁄₁₆ x 8¼.   26466-1

THE INSIDIOUS DR. FU-MANCHU, Sax Rohmer. The first of the popular mystery series introduces a pair of English detectives to their archnemesis, the diabolical Dr. Fu-Manchu. Flavorful atmosphere, fast-paced action, and colorful characters enliven this classic of the genre. 208pp. 5³⁄₁₆ x 8¼.   29898-1

THE MALLEUS MALEFICARUM OF KRAMER AND SPRENGER, translated by Montague Summers. Full text of most important witchhunter's "bible," used by both Catholics and Protestants. 278pp. 6⅝ x 10.   22802-9

SPANISH STORIES/CUENTOS ESPAÑOLES: A Dual-Language Book, Angel Flores (ed.). Unique format offers 13 great stories in Spanish by Cervantes, Borges, others. Faithful English translations on facing pages. 352pp. 5⅜ x 8½.   25399-6

GARDEN CITY, LONG ISLAND, IN EARLY PHOTOGRAPHS, 1869–1919, Mildred H. Smith. Handsome treasury of 118 vintage pictures, accompanied by carefully researched captions, document the Garden City Hotel fire (1899), the Vanderbilt Cup Race (1908), the first airmail flight departing from the Nassau Boulevard Aerodrome (1911), and much more. 96pp. 8⅞ x 11¾.   40669-5

OLD QUEENS, N.Y., IN EARLY PHOTOGRAPHS, Vincent F. Seyfried and William Asadorian. Over 160 rare photographs of Maspeth, Jamaica, Jackson Heights, and other areas. Vintage views of DeWitt Clinton mansion, 1939 World's Fair and more. Captions. 192pp. 8⅞ x 11.   26358-4

CAPTURED BY THE INDIANS: 15 Firsthand Accounts, 1750-1870, Frederick Drimmer. Astounding true historical accounts of grisly torture, bloody conflicts, relentless pursuits, miraculous escapes and more, by people who lived to tell the tale. 384pp. 5⅜ x 8½.   24901-8

THE WORLD'S GREAT SPEECHES (Fourth Enlarged Edition), Lewis Copeland, Lawrence W. Lamm, and Stephen J. McKenna. Nearly 300 speeches provide public speakers with a wealth of updated quotes and inspiration–from Pericles' funeral oration and William Jennings Bryan's "Cross of Gold Speech" to Malcolm X's powerful words on the Black Revolution and Earl of Spenser's tribute to his sister, Diana, Princess of Wales. 944pp. 5⅜ x 8⅜.   40903-1

THE BOOK OF THE SWORD, Sir Richard F. Burton. Great Victorian scholar/adventurer's eloquent, erudite history of the "queen of weapons"–from prehistory to early Roman Empire. Evolution and development of early swords, variations (sabre, broadsword, cutlass, scimitar, etc.), much more. 336pp. 6⅛ x 9¼.
25434-8

AUTOBIOGRAPHY: The Story of My Experiments with Truth, Mohandas K. Gandhi. Boyhood, legal studies, purification, the growth of the Satyagraha (nonviolent protest) movement. Critical, inspiring work of the man responsible for the freedom of India. 480pp. 5⅜ x 8½. (Available in U.S. only.) 24593-4

CELTIC MYTHS AND LEGENDS, T. W. Rolleston. Masterful retelling of Irish and Welsh stories and tales. Cuchulain, King Arthur, Deirdre, the Grail, many more. First paperback edition. 58 full-page illustrations. 512pp. 5⅜ x 8½. 26507-2

THE PRINCIPLES OF PSYCHOLOGY, William James. Famous long course complete, unabridged. Stream of thought, time perception, memory, experimental methods; great work decades ahead of its time. 94 figures. 1,391pp. 5⅜ x 8½. 2-vol. set.
Vol. I: 20381-6 Vol. II: 20382-4

THE WORLD AS WILL AND REPRESENTATION, Arthur Schopenhauer. Definitive English translation of Schopenhauer's life work, correcting more than 1,000 errors, omissions in earlier translations. Translated by E. F. J. Payne. Total of 1,269pp. 5⅜ x 8½. 2-vol. set. Vol. 1: 21761-2 Vol. 2: 21762-0

MAGIC AND MYSTERY IN TIBET, Madame Alexandra David-Neel. Experiences among lamas, magicians, sages, sorcerers, Bonpa wizards. A true psychic discovery. 32 illustrations. 321pp. 5⅜ x 8½. (Available in U.S. only.) 22682-4

THE EGYPTIAN BOOK OF THE DEAD, E. A. Wallis Budge. Complete reproduction of Ani's papyrus, finest ever found. Full hieroglyphic text, interlinear transliteration, word-for-word translation, smooth translation. 533pp. 6½ x 9¼. 21866-X

MATHEMATICS FOR THE NONMATHEMATICIAN, Morris Kline. Detailed, college-level treatment of mathematics in cultural and historical context, with numerous exercises. Recommended Reading Lists. Tables. Numerous figures. 641pp. 5⅜ x 8½.
24823-2

PROBABILISTIC METHODS IN THE THEORY OF STRUCTURES, Isaac Elishakoff. Well-written introduction covers the elements of the theory of probability from two or more random variables, the reliability of such multivariable structures, the theory of random function, Monte Carlo methods of treating problems incapable of exact solution, and more. Examples. 502pp. 5⅜ x 8½. 40691-1

THE RIME OF THE ANCIENT MARINER, Gustave Doré, S. T. Coleridge. Doré's finest work; 34 plates capture moods, subtleties of poem. Flawless full-size reproductions printed on facing pages with authoritative text of poem. "Beautiful. Simply beautiful."–*Publisher's Weekly.* 77pp. 9¼ x 12. 22305-1

NORTH AMERICAN INDIAN DESIGNS FOR ARTISTS AND CRAFTSPEOPLE, Eva Wilson. Over 360 authentic copyright-free designs adapted from Navajo blankets, Hopi pottery, Sioux buffalo hides, more. Geometrics, symbolic figures, plant and animal motifs, etc. 128pp. 8⅜ x 11. (Not for sale in the United Kingdom.) 25341-4

SCULPTURE: Principles and Practice, Louis Slobodkin. Step-by-step approach to clay, plaster, metals, stone; classical and modern. 253 drawings, photos. 255pp. 8⅛ x 11.
22960-2

THE INFLUENCE OF SEA POWER UPON HISTORY, 1660–1783, A. T. Mahan. Influential classic of naval history and tactics still used as text in war colleges. First paperback edition. 4 maps. 24 battle plans. 640pp. 5⅜ x 8½. 25509-3

THE STORY OF THE TITANIC AS TOLD BY ITS SURVIVORS, Jack Winocour (ed.). What it was really like. Panic, despair, shocking inefficiency, and a little heroism. More thrilling than any fictional account. 26 illustrations. 320pp. 5⅜ x 8½.
20610-6

FAIRY AND FOLK TALES OF THE IRISH PEASANTRY, William Butler Yeats (ed.). Treasury of 64 tales from the twilight world of Celtic myth and legend: "The Soul Cages," "The Kildare Pooka," "King O'Toole and his Goose," many more. Introduction and Notes by W. B. Yeats. 352pp. 5⅜ x 8½.
26941-8

BUDDHIST MAHAYANA TEXTS, E. B. Cowell and others (eds.). Superb, accurate translations of basic documents in Mahayana Buddhism, highly important in history of religions. The Buddha-karita of Asvaghosha, Larger Sukhavativyuha, more. 448pp. 5⅜ x 8½.
25552-2

ONE TWO THREE . . . INFINITY: Facts and Speculations of Science, George Gamow. Great physicist's fascinating, readable overview of contemporary science: number theory, relativity, fourth dimension, entropy, genes, atomic structure, much more. 128 illustrations. Index. 352pp. 5⅜ x 8½.
25664-2

EXPERIMENTATION AND MEASUREMENT, W. J. Youden. Introductory manual explains laws of measurement in simple terms and offers tips for achieving accuracy and minimizing errors. Mathematics of measurement, use of instruments, experimenting with machines. 1994 edition. Foreword. Preface. Introduction. Epilogue. Selected Readings. Glossary. Index. Tables and figures. 128pp. 5⅜ x 8½.   40451-X

DALÍ ON MODERN ART: The Cuckolds of Antiquated Modern Art, Salvador Dalí. Influential painter skewers modern art and its practitioners. Outrageous evaluations of Picasso, Cézanne, Turner, more. 15 renderings of paintings discussed. 44 calligraphic decorations by Dalí. 96pp. 5⅜ x 8½. (Available in U.S. only.)
29220-7

ANTIQUE PLAYING CARDS: A Pictorial History, Henry René D'Allemagne. Over 900 elaborate, decorative images from rare playing cards (14th–20th centuries): Bacchus, death, dancing dogs, hunting scenes, royal coats of arms, players cheating, much more. 96pp. 9¼ x 12¼.
29265-7

MAKING FURNITURE MASTERPIECES: 30 Projects with Measured Drawings, Franklin H. Gottshall. Step-by-step instructions, illustrations for constructing handsome, useful pieces, among them a Sheraton desk, Chippendale chair, Spanish desk, Queen Anne table and a William and Mary dressing mirror. 224pp. 8⅛ x 11¼.
29338-6

THE FOSSIL BOOK: A Record of Prehistoric Life, Patricia V. Rich et al. Profusely illustrated definitive guide covers everything from single-celled organisms and dinosaurs to birds and mammals and the interplay between climate and man. Over 1,500 illustrations. 760pp. 7½ x 10⅛.
29371-8

Paperbound unless otherwise indicated. Available at your book dealer, online at **www.doverpublications.com**, or by writing to Dept. GI, Dover Publications, Inc., 31 East 2nd Street, Mineola, NY 11501. For current price information or for free catalogues (please indicate field of interest), write to Dover Publications or log on to **www.doverpublications.com** and see every Dover book in print. Dover publishes more than 500 books each year on science, elementary and advanced mathematics, biology, music, art, literary history, social sciences, and other areas.